AI Made Easy:

AI Made Easy: A 7-Day Beginner's Guide to
ChatGPT and Beyond – Learn to Use AI
for Personal and Professional Growth Without
Needing Tech Skills

W.R. Lawrence

BV Publishing, LLC

© Copyright W.R. Lawrence 2024 - **All rights reserved.**

The content within this book may not be reproduced, duplicated or transmitted without direct written permission from the author or the publisher.

Under no circumstances will any blame or legal responsibility be held against the publisher, or author, for any damages, reparation, or monetary loss due to the information contained within this book. Either directly or indirectly. You are responsible for your own choices, actions, and results.

Legal Notice:

This book is copyright protected. This book is only for personal use. You cannot amend, distribute, sell, use, quote or paraphrase any part, of the content within this book, without the consent of the author or publisher.

Disclaimer Notice:

Please note the information contained within this document is for educational and entertainment purposes only. All effort has been expended to present accurate, up-to-date, and reliable, complete information. No warranties of any kind are declared or implied. Readers acknowledge that the author is not engaging in the rendering of legal, financial, medical or professional advice. The content within this book has been derived from various sources. Please consult a licensed professional before attempting any techniques outlined in this book.

By reading this document, the reader agrees that under no circumstances is the author responsible for any losses, direct or indirect, which are incurred as a result of the use of the information contained within this document, including, but not limited to, — errors, omissions, or inaccuracies.

Contents

Introduction VI

1. Understanding AI and ChatGPT Basics 1
    1.1 What is Artificial Intelligence? Beyond Sci-Fi
    1.2 Decoding ChatGPT: Your AI Communication Partner
    1.4 Understanding Neural Networks: The Brain Behind AI
    1.5 Key AI Concepts Explained with Everyday Analogies
    1.6 Navigating AI Jargon: A Beginner's Glossary
    1.7 Five AI & ChatGPT Mistakes Beginners Should Avoid
    Chapter 1- Exercises

2. Welcome to the Digital Dojo: Your Guide to Becoming a ChatGPT Master! 17
    2.1 Getting Started with ChatGPT: Installation and Setup
    2.2 Your First Chat with ChatGPT: A Walkthrough
    2.3 Customizing ChatGPT Settings for Optimal Use
    2.4 Essential ChatGPT Commands You Should Know
    2.5 Troubleshooting Common ChatGPT Issues
    2.6 Enhancing Privacy and Security When Using ChatGPT
    Chapter 2 - Exercises

3. Practical Applications of AI and ChatGPT: Making ChatGPT Your Own 29
    3.1 Integrating ChatGPT in Daily Personal Tasks
    3.2 Using AI for Enhanced Content Creation
    3.3 Managing Money With AI

3.4 ChatGPT for Learning

   3.5 Organizing Your Life with AI

   3.6 Creative Writing with AI: Composing Poetry and Stories

   3.7 Creating Images with AI: A Beginner's Guide

   3.8 AI in Video Creation and Editing

   3.9 AI in Music and Sound Creation

   3.10 AI in Personal Health and Fitness

   3.11 AI in Shopping and Fashion

   3.12 AI in Smart Assistants and Voice Technology

   3.13 AI in Education and Learning

   Chapter 3 Exercises: Practical Applications of AI and ChatGPT

   Outcome Section: Chapter 3 Exercises

4. AI in the Professional Sphere — 55

   4.1 Automating Routine Tasks with AI in the Office

   4.2 AI Tools for Data Analysis and Decision Making

   4.3 Enhancing Customer Service with ChatGPT

   4.4 Using AI for Project Management: A Game Changer

   4.5 Networking and Building Professional Relationships with AI

   4.6 AI Ethics in the Workplace: What You Need to Know

   Chapter 4 Exercises:

Make a Difference with Your Review — 69

5. Hands-On Projects and Exercises — 71

   5.1 Creating Your First AI Chatbot

   5.2 Designing a Simple AI-Driven Survey

   5.3 Build a Resume Analyzer Using ChatGPT

   5.4 Setting Up an AI-Powered Reminder System

   5.5 Exercise: Generate a Marketing Campaign with AI

   5.6 Project: Automate Email Responses with ChatGPT

6. Addressing Ethical Considerations — 93

   6.1 Understanding AI Bias and How to Mitigate It

   6.2 Privacy Concerns with AI: What You Should Know

   6.3 The Future of AI: Ethical Considerations and Predictions

   6.4 Transparency in AI: Why It Matters

      6.5 Misuse of AI: A Critical Issue

      6.6 Ethical AI Usage: Best Practices for Beginners

      Exercises for Chapter 6: Addressing Ethical Considerations

7. Keeping Up with AI Developments   104

      7.1 Following AI Innovations: Best Sources and Practices

      7.2 Participating in AI and ChatGPT Online Communities

      7.3 Continuous Learning in AI: Online Courses and Resources

      7.4 Conferences and Workshops on AI You Should Not Miss

      7.5 Reading List: Essential Books on AI for Continuous Learning

      7.6 The Role of Podcasts in AI Education

      Chapter 7 Exercises:

8. Leveraging AI for Future Opportunities   120

      8.1 Career Paths in AI and Machine Learning

      8.2 Starting Your Own AI Business

      8.3 AI for Lifelong Learning and Personal Growth

      8.4 How AI Is Shaping the Future of Industries

      8.5: Preparing for a Future Dominated by AI

      8.6 Embracing AI: Next Steps in Your AI Journey

      Chapter 8 - Exercises

Keeping the Learning Alive   135

9. AI Made Easy: Conclusion   136

10. AI Workbook: Using AI in Everyday Tech Devices   138

11. References   148

Introduction

Have you ever sat at your computer, staring at the screen, wondering if AI is just a fancy calculator? You're not alone. Many feel overwhelmed by the hype and jargon, thinking it's only for tech experts. But that's where I come in.

Hi, I'm W.R. Lawrence. After years of exploring AI, I've made it my mission to help beginners like you navigate this exciting world. My book is your 7-day guide to using AI in your daily life and at work. We'll explore creative AI tools like ChatGPT and DALL-E, showing how AI can be your partner in everything from composing poetry to creating images. Even if tech isn't your thing, you'll discover how AI can turn daunting tasks into simple, enjoyable experiences.

Why seven days? Because this book is structured to provide step-by-step, easy-to-understand learning chunks. Each day, you'll engage in interactive exercises to build your confidence in using AI. By the end of this guide, what once seemed like a scary world of codes and algorithms will feel like a handy toolkit—a set of skills you can use to make your workday smoother and your personal life a bit less hectic.

Throughout this journey, you'll discover how AI can improve your email automation, personalize your browsing experience, and optimize your smartphone use. You'll learn to use AI assistants to manage your schedule, control smart home devices, and even create personalized greeting cards. Each day's activities are designed to seamlessly integrate AI into your routine, transforming complex tasks into simple, efficient processes.

If you're worried about diving into technology, don't be. This book is written specifically for beginners. You don't need any tech expertise here—just bring your curiosity, and I'll help you with the rest.

We'll also talk about the ethical side of AI, making sure you use these tools responsibly. It's important to me—and should be to you—that we use AI in a way that benefits everyone.

By the end of this journey, AI will feel less like a buzzword and more like a tool that makes your everyday tasks—from email drafting to video editing—a whole lot easier.

Ready to dive in? Let's make AI your creative and practical ally.

Chapter One

Understanding AI and ChatGPT Basics

CHAPTER 1

So, you've decided to learn about Artificial Intelligence or (AI). Great choice! Let me clear up any worries you might have about AI being a sci-fi movie villain planning to take over the world. AI is more like the helpful robot in those movies that give advice or, in real life, helps you find the fastest route to your next meeting or suggests what to cook for dinner.

In this chapter, we will explain AI and ChatGPT basics. I'll walk you through what AI is (hint: it's not just robots), how it's becoming part of almost every tech you use today, and why understanding it isn't just for tech geniuses. Whether you want to use AI to boost your startup, manage your schedule, or just sound smart at parties, you're in the right place. Let's start with some foundational knowledge that will make the rest of your AI adventure easy.

***

1.1 What is Artificial Intelligence? Beyond Sci-Fi

Let's start with the basics: Artificial Intelligence is a fancy term for machines that act like humans. Imagine your smartphone turning off the lights at home or your car warning you about traffic on your route before you ask. That's AI in action. It's not about machines plotting world domination but about making your coffee maker smart enough to have it ready when you wake up.

AI ranges from simple machines that can perform tasks like automatically sorting your emails to complex systems like neural networks, which are a bit like a brain for computers. These systems learn and adapt from the information they process, just like how you learn to avoid that one squeaky floorboard at night. This ability to perform tasks and learn from them sets AI apart from other forms of technology.

Now, let's bust some myths. Despite what many sci-fi films show, AI isn't capable of achieving its goals (like world domination), nor is it likely to replace all human jobs. What AI does well is handle repetitive tasks, analyze large datasets quickly, and help us understand patterns we can't easily see ourselves. It's a tool, not a replacement for human creativity and decision-making.

The story of AI began in the mid-20th century with visionaries who believed machines could simulate human intelligence. From simple algorithms in the 1950s, AI has become a crucial part of daily technology, powering everything from personal assistants like Siri and Alexa to recommendation systems on Netflix and Amazon that suggest what you should watch or buy next.

***

The AI Timeline

Here's a timeline showing the key moments in AI history, from the Turing Test to the latest developments, helping you see how AI has evolved.

- 1950s: The Dawn of AI

    - 1950: Alan Turing publishes "Computing Machinery and Intelligence," introducing the concept of the Turing Test.

    - 1956: The term "Artificial Intelligence" is coined at the Dartmouth Conference by John McCarthy, Marvin Minsky, Nathaniel Rochester, and Claude Shannon.

- 1960s: Early Developments

    - 1961: IBM's 1401, the first mass-produced computer, uses assembly language for business data processing.

    - 1966: Joseph Weizenbaum creates ELIZA, an early natural language processing computer program.

- 1970s: The First AI Winter

    - 1972: The logic programming language PROLOG is created.

    - 1973: The Lighthill Report criticizes AI research, leading to reduced funding in the UK.

- 1980s: Expert Systems and Second AI Boom

- 1980: Introduction of the first expert system, XCON, by Digital Equipment Corporation.

- 1986: Geoffrey Hinton, David Rumelhart, and Ronald Williams popularize back-propagation, a key algorithm for training neural networks.1990s: Advancements and Real-world Applications

- 1997: IBM's Deep Blue defeats world chess champion Garry Kasparov.

- 1999: Launch of Sony's AIBO, an AI-powered robotic pet.

- <u>2000s: Rise of Machine Learning</u>

- 2006: Geoffrey Hinton and Ruslan Salakhutdinov introduce deep belief networks.

- 2009: Google begins developing its self-driving car project.

- 2010s: AI in Everyday Life

- 2011: IBM Watson wins Jeopardy! against former champions Brad Rutter and Ken Jennings.

- 2012: AlexNet, a deep convolutional neural network, wins the ImageNet Large Scale Visual Recognition Challenge.

- 2014: Google acquires DeepMind, an AI research lab.

- 2016: AlphaGo, developed by DeepMind, defeats Go champion Lee Sedol.

- <u>2020s: AI in the Modern Era</u>

- 2020: OpenAI releases GPT-3, a state-of-the-art language model.

- 2021: DeepMind's AlphaFold2 makes significant advances in protein folding predictions.

- 2023: GPT-4, a more advanced language model by OpenAI, is released.

Understanding AI is the first step in clarifying its role in your life. It's not about the machines taking over; it's about how these intelligent tools are here to make your life easier and your work more productive. As we peel back the layers of AI throughout this chapter, you'll see how much of it is already interwoven into your daily routines and how it can be a powerful tool in your arsenal.

Whether sorting your emails, helping you navigate through traffic, or suggesting what to cook for dinner, AI enhances your efficiency and enables you to manage your day-to-day tasks more effectively.

1.2 Decoding ChatGPT: Your AI Communication Partner

Let's talk about one of AI's coolest creations, ChatGPT. Imagine you had a buddy who knew almost everything, could chat in any language, and even help you write your emails. Sounds awesome, right? That's what ChatGPT is like, except it can't fetch you coffee. ChatGPT is an AI developed by OpenAI and is part of the GPT (Generative Pre-trained Transformer) family. This smart tool is designed to generate text that sounds like a human wrote it – which is pretty amazing and a bit spooky when you think about it.

So, how does ChatGPT work? It's all about patterns and data. ChatGPT has been fed (not with food, but with data) tons of text from books, websites, and all over the internet. It uses this data to find patterns and understand how words and phrases naturally fit together. When you ask ChatGPT a question or give it a prompt, it uses this understanding to generate responses that are accurate and make sense. Think of it as having a super-smart pen pal who has read way more books than you ever will.

The uses for ChatGPT are really impressive. In customer service, it's like the best helper ever, giving quick, informative, and polite responses 24/7, making sure customer questions are always answered, no matter the time of day. In education, teachers use ChatGPT to create custom learning materials, making interactive and adaptive learning experiences that can fit each student's needs. Then there's content creation, where ChatGPT helps writers get over writer's block by suggesting text, generating draft articles, or even writing code. It's like having a brainstorming buddy who's always ready to help.

You need to know a few tricks to get the best results when talking to ChatGPT. It's like learning to speak to a new friend who takes things very literally. Your questions must be clear and specific. Vague questions get vague answers. If you're too broad, like asking, "Tell me something interesting," you might get a fact about frog mating rituals when you want a quick update on the stock market. Being precise in your questions makes a big difference. Also, remember that ChatGPT, as smart as it is, doesn't "know" things like humans do – it gives information based on patterns, so always double-check important facts.

Wondering how to start using this nifty tool? It's easier than you think. Whether you want to streamline your work tasks, boost your learning, or just have fun with AI,

ChatGPT is like a Swiss Army knife in your digital toolkit. It's ready to help – just type in a prompt (a specific input or question) to get a response. As you get more familiar with the kinds of prompts that work best, you'll find ChatGPT becomes a vital part of your daily digital life. So, ask it to draft an email, explain quantum physics, or even tell you a joke. ChatGPT is here to make your life easier and a bit more fun.

1.3 How AI and ChatGPT Learn: An Overview of Machine Learning

Let's roll up our sleeves and dive into how AI, especially our buddy ChatGPT, learns to do its magic. Imagine you're trying to teach your dog a new trick. You wouldn't just give it a bunch of instructions all at once and expect it to jump through hoops. No, you break it down into steps, using treats (data) to guide it through each part (algorithms), rewarding it as it gets closer to what you want. In simple terms, this is what machine learning in AI looks like.

Machine learning is the backbone of AI. It's all about teaching machines to understand data and make decisions based on it. Unlike traditional programming, where every single command must be written out, machine learning lets machines learn from data patterns and make decisions on their own. It's like teaching them to think (or at least act like they're thinking) on their feet.

Now, let's talk about how ChatGPT gets trained. Imagine you have a giant cookbook with every recipe ever made. ChatGPT's training process involves feeding it a massive amount of text data from various sources like books, websites, and newspapers. This is where it starts to understand language patterns and context. But how do we make sure it doesn't give you a Shakespearean speech when you just want to know how to boil an egg? This is where fine-tuning comes in. Developers fine-tune ChatGPT by training it on specific data types, helping it become better at certain tasks, like translating languages or writing articles.

Now, let's talk about supervised vs. unsupervised learning, which sounds like something from a sci-fi movie. Supervised learning is like training wheels on a bicycle—it guides AI with labeled data, showing it exactly what to learn. For example, when training ChatGPT, if you give it a conversation labeled as a customer service chat, it learns to recognize and generate similar responses. On the other hand, unsupervised learning is like taking off the training wheels. Here, AI is given data without clear instructions on what to learn. It has to figure out patterns and relationships within the data by itself. While

ChatGPT mainly learns from the supervised method, understanding both is important in AI.

Let's not forget about the quality and amount of data. Just like a bad diet can affect your health, poor-quality data can lead AI in the wrong direction. AI systems can pick up biases from their training data, which can result in unfair outcomes. For example, if ChatGPT is trained on texts that only describe engineers as male, it might generate biased content. Feeding AI with diverse, accurate, and large amounts of data is like providing a balanced diet for your pet; it helps them grow healthy and smart.

Understanding these basics of how AI learns helps make this complex technology less scary. It's not about creating an all-knowing oracle but rather training a system that can handle tasks that mimic human intelligence using data and patterns. This understanding makes AI less intimidating and shows how it can be used effectively in everyday situations, ensuring the technology works for us, not against us.

1.4 Understanding Neural Networks: The Brain Behind AI

Imagine that your brain is a busy city, with information zipping around like taxis during rush hour. This is a good way to start understanding neural networks. In AI, neural networks are like the smart brains behind the scenes. They are inspired by how our brains work and are made up of layers of nodes, similar to neurons. This is where the magic of AI happens, as these networks learn from the large amounts of data they are given.

So, what exactly is a neural network? Think of it as a series of connected nodes, or artificial neurons, each layer doing specific tasks. Information enters through the input layer, moves through hidden layers where the processing happens, and comes out through the output layer with the final result. Each node in these layers is like a mini decision-maker, doing simple calculations and passing on the results. The real power comes from the connections between these nodes, which can get stronger or weaker over time, making the network better at making accurate predictions or decisions.

The layers in neural networks add different levels of complexity. For example, the first layer recognizes simple details, like edges, in an image. As data moves through the layers, the network gets better at remembering more complex features, like shapes. By the final layer, the network can understand sophisticated concepts, like identifying faces in images. This step-by-step learning process helps neural networks work well with large and complicated datasets, and they get better as they process more data.

Neural networks are crucial in many AI applications, especially natural language processing (NLP). This technology powers everything from your email's spam filter to Siri's ability to understand your requests. Each word or phrase you input is broken down into data the neural network uses to learn and predict future inputs. This is why your virtual assistant gets smarter over time, better understands your commands, and even guesses what you might need next.

To help you picture how data moves and changes within a neural network, imagine watching a sports game and wanting your AI system to predict the winning team based on past performance data. The input layer includes the raw data, like team statistics and game conditions. The hidden layers analyze this data by looking at patterns and relationships, such as how a team performs under different conditions. By the time it reaches the output layer, the neural network has processed the information to predict which team will likely win based on the learned data and patterns.

***

Visual Aid: Diagram of Neural Network Operations

Here's a diagram of a simple neural network with its layers. You can see how data goes in through the input layer, gets worked on in the hidden layers, and then comes out as a result at the output layer. It's like putting ingredients into a blender. What comes out is a mix influenced by how all the ingredients combine inside.

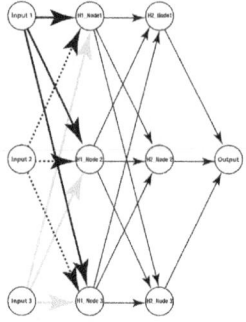

Understanding neural networks and how they work helps you see how AI applications get smart. It's like looking under the hood of a car; you might not need to know every detail to drive it, but it helps when you're trying to figure out why it's making a weird noise. For AI, knowing about neural networks helps you understand how machines learn from data and improve over time. This turns what might seem like alien technology into useful everyday tools that help with things like translating languages or suggesting your next favorite book. As we keep exploring AI, understanding neural networks will help you see what AI can do in different fields, like healthcare or customer service, making technology work smarter for us all.

***

1.5 Key AI Concepts Explained with Everyday Analogies

Let's break down some key AI concepts using everyday examples that anyone can understand. You don't need a PhD in Computer Science to get artificial intelligence! So, let's dive in and stir some knowledge into our AI soup.

Algorithms: The Recipes of AI

If AI were a kitchen, algorithms would be the recipes. Imagine you're making your favorite cookies. You have a recipe that tells you exactly what you need: two cups of flour, one cup of sugar, a dash of vanilla, and so on. You follow these step-by-step instructions to combine the ingredients and bake them at the right temperature. Hopefully, you get a delicious batch of cookies! Algorithms in AI work the same way. They are instructions that tell the computer to take specific inputs (like data) and turn them into outputs (like predictions or decisions). Like in cooking, the quality of your output (cookies or AI predictions) depends on how well your recipe (algorithm) is and how well you follow it.

Training AI: Like Teaching a Child

Training AI is like teaching a child. When you teach a child to recognize animals, you show them pictures of different animals and name each one. "This is a cat," you say, pointing to a picture of a cat. Through repetition and correction, the child learns to connect the image of the cat with the word "cat." Each time they correctly identify the cat, they get better, and if they make a mistake, you help them learn from it. Training AI is similar. You give the AI system lots of data (like showing a child many pictures). Some of this data is used for training, where the AI makes guesses and learns from its mistakes. The more good quality data the AI is trained on, the better it gets at making predictions and functioning, just like the more examples a child sees, the better they become at recognizing animals.

Neural Networks: The Team of Experts

Imagine a neural network as a team of experts. Each "expert" or node in the network handles a specific part of a problem. For example, in a team working to solve a complex business issue, one expert might analyze the financial aspects, another might look at market trends, and another might examine customer feedback. They each assess and pass their insights to the next expert. Finally, all these insights are combined to make a well-rounded decision. Neural networks work similarly. Information is processed layer by layer, with each layer handling different parts of the data, gradually leading to a final decision or output. This teamwork makes neural networks incredibly effective for tasks like recognizing images or understanding speech, where different layers learn to identify various data elements.

Imagine a neural network as a team of experts. Each "expert" or node in the network specializes in handling a specific part of a problem. For instance, in a team working to solve a complex business issue, one expert might analyze the financial aspects, another might look at the market trends, and another might examine the customer feedback. They each assess and pass their insights on to the next expert in the line. Finally, all these insights are compiled to form a well-rounded decision. Neural networks operate similarly. Information is processed layer by layer, each handling different parts of the data, gradually leading to a final decision or output. This collaborative filtering and processing make neural networks incredibly effective for tasks like image and speech recognition, where different layers can learn to identify various data elements.

***

Bias in AI: Like Human Judgment

Just as people can have biases based on their experiences, upbringing, or the information they've been exposed to, AI systems can develop biases based on the data they are trained on. If an AI system is trained on data that is not diverse or is skewed in a certain way, it will develop a 'prejudice' that reflects that data. For example, if a hiring AI is mainly trained on resumes from a particular demographic, it may favor candidates from that demographic. It's not because the AI is inherently prejudiced but because it mirrors the limitations and biases in the training data. Just like human prejudice can lead to unfair or harmful decisions, AI bias can lead to inaccurate or unfair outputs. Recognizing and correcting these biases is crucial in developing fair and effective AI systems.

Understanding these AI concepts through simple analogies helps explain the technology. AI is based on processes we're familiar with in our everyday lives. By comparing these concepts to cooking, teaching children, teamwork, and human biases, we see that AI is about patterns, learning, collaboration, and the need for diverse and accurate information. Whether it's deciding on what movie to watch next or analyzing complex data to predict market trends, AI's capabilities are vast and varied. Still, the principles behind them are easy to relate to. This understanding makes AI less intimidating and highlights the importance of thoughtfully designing and training AI systems to serve us effectively and ethically.

1.6 Navigating AI Jargon: A Beginner's Glossary

Welcome to the linguistic labyrinth of AI—where words like "neural network" and "algorithm" are tossed around like confetti at a techie parade. Fear not! I'm here to be your glossary guru, turning the jargon jungle into a stroll through a well-mapped park. Let's decode some of these terms with plain speak that even my non-techie Aunt Marge could grasp over her Sunday roast.

First up, let's tackle "deep learning." Picture this: you're learning to play the guitar. At first, you memorize chords and their finger placements (that's your basic learning). But then, as you start to understand how chords form a song, you begin experimenting with strumming patterns and rhythms, developing a deeper understanding of music. Deep learning in AI works similarly—it's a type of machine learning. Still, it involves more profound processing layers, allowing the machine to make sense of complex patterns. This is how services like Google Photos can recognize your friend's face in a photo from a concert years ago amidst the crowd. The system has learned from numerous images to distinguish facial features at a profoundly intricate level.

Next, let's clarify "natural language processing" or NLP. Have you ever yelled at your digital assistant because it played jazz when you asked for classic rock? That's NLP in action, albeit a bit flustered. NLP is how machines understand and respond to human language. The goal is for your AI assistant to recognize words and understand your intent, so whether you're asking for weather updates or the latest rock hits, it gets it right. It's like teaching your dog to fetch slippers instead of a squeaky toy; it needs to understand the difference between your lounging needs and playtime.

Now, on to "neural network." If AI were a brain, the neural network would be its neural pathways. These networks are layers upon layers of algorithms that mimic the human brain's structure and function. Each layer has nodes, like tiny brains, that work on specific pieces of a task. For example, in recognizing a voice command, one layer might focus on detecting sounds, another on interpreting these sounds as words, and another might determine the command's intent. It's teamwork on a microscopic scale, with each layer passing its findings to the next, refining the output step by step until the AI understands that when you say, "Play some rock," you don't mean geology lectures on YouTube.

Finally, the good old "algorithm," the bread and butter of AI. An algorithm is a set of step-by-step instructions for solving a problem or performing a task. Imagine you're writing down a recipe for your famous chili. The recipe is your algorithm; it tells someone what ingredients they need and the steps to cook them to replicate your culinary masterpiece. In AI, algorithms process data and make decisions based on the programmed instructions. So, when Netflix suggests a new series, it's not magic—it's an algorithm analyzing your previous viewing habits to predict what might keep you binge-watching.

Now, why should you care about getting cozy with these terms? As you dip your toes deeper into the AI waters, these terms will help you navigate the tech talks.

Knowing this lingo is key whether you're trying to impress at a job interview, decode a tech article, or understand what your smart fridge is doing.

If you're eager to learn more, don't stop here. Check out resources like the online AI Dictionary for Non-Scientists or platforms like Khan Academy and Coursera, which offer easy-to-understand courses and explanations. These tools will help you learn more words and understand how AI technologies are changing the world around us.

As we finish this tour of AI language, remember that every field has its special words. Just like you wouldn't become an expert in wine tasting or car mechanics overnight, learning AI's language takes time. But with a bit of patience and curiosity, you'll soon be confidently talking about neural networks and algorithms. Keep exploring, keep learning, and let AI amaze you with what it can do. Every expert started as a beginner, and every professional was once a novice. So, let these words be stepping stones, not obstacles, as you explore the exciting world of artificial intelligence.

1.7 Five AI & ChatGPT Mistakes Beginners Should Avoid

Thinking AI is Perfect

Many beginners believe that AI, like ChatGPT, can understand everything perfectly and do anything. This isn't true. AI has limitations and can make mistakes. It is important to have realistic expectations and understand that AI is not perfect.

Ignoring Good Data

AI learns from data, so good, clean data is important. The AI won't learn properly if the data is messy or incorrect. Beginners often overlook this and don't realize how crucial good data is for teaching AI.

Skipping Basics

Understanding basic concepts about AI, like how it learns and understands language, is essential. Beginners sometimes skip these fundamentals and jump into advanced topics too quickly, which can lead to confusion and mistakes.

Not Trying Different Things

Experimenting with different questions and models helps you understand how AI works and what it can do. Beginners often stick to one way of doing things and miss out on learning from trying new approaches.

Forgetting About Ethics

AI can have biases and make decisions that aren't fair or ethical. Beginners often forget to think about these issues. It's important to consider the moral implications and ensure AI is used responsibly.

Chapter 1- Exercises

Completing these exercises will help you understand the basics of AI and ChatGPT, making the technology easier to use in your everyday life.

Exercise 1: AI in Everyday Life

Objective: Find real-world examples of AI in your daily routine.
   Instructions:
   1. Think about your daily activities and list five times you encounter AI. These could be as simple as using a smartphone app or as complex as interacting with a virtual assistant.
   2. For each example, describe how AI is being used and what benefits it provides.

Exercise 2: Debunking AI Myths

Objective: Separate fact from fiction regarding common AI myths.
   Instructions:
   Read the following statements and decide if they are true or false.
- AI can think and feel like humans.
- AI is designed to replace all human jobs.
- AI systems can learn from data without human help.
- AI is only used in high-tech industries.

Exercise 3: Ethical Considerations in AI

Objective: Think about the ethical issues related to AI technology.
   Instructions:

1. Find a recent news story involving AI that raised ethical concerns. This could be about privacy, bias, job loss, or other issues
2. Summarize the story and point out the main ethical issues involved.

***

Exercise 4: Avoiding Common AI & ChatGPT Mistakes

Objective: Learn about and avoid common mistakes beginners make when learning about AI and ChatGPT.

Instructions:

Complete these activities on your own to understand the five common mistakes and how to avoid them.

Activities:

1. **Thinking AI is Perfect:**

- **Task**: Write a short story where AI makes a funny mistake. This will help you see that AI isn't perfect.

- **Reflection**: Consider why it's important to know that AI can make mistakes. Write down your thoughts in a paragraph.

1. **Ignoring Good Data:**

- **Task:** Find two datasets online—one clean and one messy. Run simple AI tasks on both datasets to see how the quality of data affects results (you can use free tools or platforms like Google Colab)

- **Reflection:** Write a paragraph about why having good, clean data is important for AI learning.

1. **Skipping Basics:**

- **Task:** Make a mind map of basic AI ideas like machine learning, neural networks, and natural language processing. You can use online tools like Mind-

Meister or draw it on paper.

- **Quiz:** Find a simple online quiz about basic AI concepts and take it to strengthen your understanding.

1. **Not Trying Different Things:**

- **Task**: Ask ChatGPT five different types of questions (e.g., factual, creative, personal, hypothetical, and instructional). Notice the differences in responses.

- **Journal**: Write a short journal entry about what you learned from asking different questions and how it helps you understand AI better.

1. **Forgetting About Ethics:**

- **Task**: Research a real-life story where AI made an unethical decision. Write a summary of what happened and why it was a problem.

- **Ethics Checklist**: Create a checklist of things to consider to make sure AI is used ethically.

Conclusion:

Think about what you learned from these activities and write a brief summary. Keep this summary for future reference as you continue learning about AI.

Chapter Two

Welcome to the Digital Dojo: Your Guide to Becoming a ChatGPT Master!

Welcome to the digital dojo! Here, you'll train to become a ChatGPT master. Think of this chapter as your techie boot camp, designed to take you from beginner to proficient ChatGPT user. Whether you want to automate tasks, craft cool emails, or impress friends with your AI assistant, getting started with ChatGPT is your first step to a smarter digital life. So, buckle up, and let's get 'techy'!

***

2.1 Getting Started with ChatGPT: Installation and Setup

Choosing the Right Platform

ChatGPT is like a chameleon; it works on various platforms to fit your tech lifestyle. You can use it through web interfaces, perfect if you don't want extra apps on your device. Just open any standard web browser, type in the address, click, and start chatting.

There are also dedicated apps for Android and iOS, which are great for using ChatGPT on the go. These apps come with extra features like push notifications and offline use, which are handy when you're in a subway tunnel and want to chat with your AI buddy.

For the more tech-savvy, ChatGPT can be integrated into other services via APIs (Application Programming Interfaces). This means you can embed ChatGPT into your websites or apps, allowing it to chat with visitors or help sort customer queries. The possibilities are endless!

Installation Process

Installing ChatGPT is super easy—easier than baking a pie! If you're using the web, no installation is needed. Just visit the website, sign in, and start chatting. For apps, go to your app store, search for ChatGPT, and download it. It's free, and within minutes, you'll have a new AI friend on your smartphone.

If you run into issues, like the app not downloading or the website not loading, don't panic! First, check your internet connection—AI can't fix spotty Wi-Fi. If that's not the problem, make sure your device's operating system is up to date. Sometimes, a quick update or restart can solve the issue.

Initial Configuration

Before you can use ChatGPT fully, you'll need to tweak some settings. It's like setting up a new phone; you want it just right for your needs. When you first start ChatGPT, go into the settings menu. Here, you can change the language settings—ChatGPT can speak multiple languages!

Setting your time zone is also important, especially if you plan to use ChatGPT for scheduling or reminders. You don't want a reminder for a meeting that happened two hours ago because your AI was in a different time zone!

Account Creation and Management

Creating an account with ChatGPT is simple. Enter your email, create a password, and maybe go through a verification process to prove you're not a robot (ironic, right?). Once your account is set up, explore the user profile settings. You can manage preferences, adjust privacy settings, and customize how ChatGPT interacts with you.

Keeping your account updated is important. AI evolves fast, and updating your app ensures you have the latest features and bug fixes for a smooth chatting experience.

Now, you're ready to dive deeper into the world of AI chatting! With each step, setting adjustment, and chat, you're getting better at using ChatGPT. Keep exploring, tweaking, and, most importantly, chatting!

2.2 Your First Chat with ChatGPT: A Walkthrough

So, you've got ChatGPT installed and you're ready to chat. What's next? It's time to craft your first input, and I promise, it's more fun than picking a movie on Netflix. Think of ChatGPT as a new friend who's super smart. To get the most out of this digital buddy, you must know how to ask questions or make statements effectively. It's like learning the right way to toss a ball to have a good game of catch.

Start with clear, concise inputs. If your question is too vague, like "Tell me something," ChatGPT might give you a random answer. Instead, be specific. Ask, "What's the weather like in New York today?" or "Can you explain Newton's first law of motion?" This way, you guide ChatGPT to give you the right information.

Understanding how ChatGPT crafts its responses is like figuring out a magic trick. Here's the secret: it's all about the model's training. ChatGPT has read tons of text from various sources, learning patterns in data, language nuances, and the context of words. When you ask a question, it doesn't just look up an answer. Instead, it generates a response based on patterns it has learned. It's like learning to cook by watching others and then trying it yourself rather than just following recipes word for word.

Now, let's make your chats with ChatGPT more engaging. Talk to it as if you're texting a friend who gives great advice, solves math problems, or explains complex topics like quantum physics in simple terms. This conversational exchange helps ChatGPT understand the context better and provide more accurate responses. For example, if you're planning a trip and need to know the weather, start with "What's the weather like in Paris today?" Based on the response, you might follow up with, "What about this weekend?" This back-and-forth keeps the context clear and helps ChatGPT track the conversation.

Experimenting with ChatGPT can be as fun as trying out a new recipe. Mix things up with different requests to see what this AI can do. Ask for a joke, then switch to getting a summary of the latest news. Try asking for a poem about the moon, or if you're feeling adventurous, see if it can help draft a heartfelt apology or a fun birthday greeting. Each interaction will give you insights into ChatGPT's flexibility and range. The more you play around with different prompts, the better you'll understand what types of questions or tasks ChatGPT handles best.

As you spend more time chatting with ChatGPT, you'll see it less like a tool and more like a partner in your quest for information, creativity, or just good old entertainment. It's like chatting with someone who is encyclopedia-smart, always awake, and endlessly patient, ready to tackle any question you can think of. So go ahead, type away, and discover how ChatGPT can make life easier and more fun!

2.3 Customizing ChatGPT Settings for Optimal Use

When you start exploring all the cool stuff ChatGPT can do, it can be super exciting! But to get the most out of it, you need to tweak the settings to fit your style and needs. Think of it like adjusting your car's seat and mirrors before a long drive—making the ride comfortable, efficient, and enjoyable. Let's dive into how you can tweak ChatGPT settings to create a more personalized interaction experience.

Personalizing ChatGPT

To make ChatGPT your own, you can adjust how chatty it is. Do you know how annoying it can be when someone talks too much or too little? ChatGPT can change its response length to fit your preference. Whether you want a quick reply or a detailed explanation, you can set it up just right. You can also adjust the complexity of responses. If you like simple answers or enjoy detailed descriptions, you can tweak ChatGPT to meet your curiosity.

Boosting Efficiency

Everyone loves being efficient. Setting up shortcuts and macros can save you a lot of time, especially when repeatedly dealing with the same questions or commands. Imagine you're working on a project and need updates from various data sources, or you're in customer service and often respond to standard queries. Creating shortcuts for these frequent commands saves time and effort. It's like having speed dial for your most-used ChatGPT functions—just a few taps, and you're there!

Language and Accessibility Settings

If English isn't your first language or you're learning a new one, adjusting the language settings is crucial. ChatGPT can interact in multiple languages, making it great for practice or ensuring you get information in the language you're most comfortable with. For users with disabilities, tweaking accessibility settings is important. Features like voice-to-text or text-to-voice can significantly enhance usability, making sure ChatGPT is a tool for everyone, regardless of language proficiency or physical ability.

Feedback Mechanisms

Giving feedback to ChatGPT is like having a direct line to improve your digital assistant. Just like you would give feedback at a restaurant, you can let ChatGPT know what you loved or what could be better. If a response misses the mark, providing feedback helps refine ChatGPT's accuracy and relevance. Over time, this makes your AI companion smarter and more in tune with your preferences and interaction style. It's a win-win: ChatGPT learns to serve you better, and you get a more customized experience.

Customizing ChatGPT is not just about tweaking technical settings. It's about shaping ChatGPT to fit seamlessly into your daily life, enhancing your interactions, and ensuring every exchange is as informative, efficient, and enjoyable as possible. Whether for work, learning, or fun, these adjustments can transform ChatGPT from a generic tool into your personalized digital assistant. So, take the time to explore these settings, adjust as you go, and continually refine how you interact with this powerful tool. After all, the goal is to make technology work for you, not vice versa.

2.4 Essential ChatGPT Commands You Should Know

Navigating ChatGPT can sometimes feel like you're trying to learn a new language. But don't worry! Just as you wouldn't go hiking without a map, you shouldn't dive into ChatGPT without knowing some basic commands. These commands ensure that every interaction with ChatGPT goes smoothly. Think of this as your cheat sheet to becoming a ChatGPT expert.

Basic Commands

Let's start with the basics. Every user should know how to start a conversation, make specific requests, and end the chat. For instance, beginning with a simple "Hello" or "Hi there!" sets a friendly tone. Follow this with what you need, like, "Can you help me understand quantum mechanics?" Yes, it can handle that! Closing with a "Thank you" or "That's all for now" wraps up the session neatly, just like in a real conversation.

Advanced Commands

Now, let's move on to something more exciting: advanced commands. These are not everyday commands but are super handy when you need ChatGPT to perform specific tasks. Say you're working on a project and need information in a structured format. You might use a command like, "Format this information into a bullet-point list." Suddenly, you're not just getting raw data; you're getting information ready to be used in your presentation or report. Or, if you're a developer needing code examples, you could write a prompt like, "Show me an example of a Python function for sorting a list." It's like having a coding buddy right there with you!

Using Commands Efficiently

Knowing when to use these commands can be a game-changer. Imagine you're planning a road trip and need a quick list of car rental options, places to visit, and weather conditions. Combining basic and advanced commands can streamline your planning process. Start with, "What are the best car rental services in Los Angeles?" followed by, "List the top 5 tourist attractions," and "What's the weather forecast for next week?" In minutes, you've got a personalized travel planner at your fingertips.

Practice Makes Perfect

Now for the fun part—practice exercises to get these commands down pat. Think of it like being a chef trying out recipes in a kitchen. The more you practice, the better your dishes turn out. It's the same with mastering ChatGPT commands. Start easy: ask ChatGPT to switch an introductory sentence from active to passive voice or summarize a paragraph. Once you're comfortable, try something more challenging, like asking for a brief write-up on a historical event or a step-by-step guide on a DIY project. Each task you perform with ChatGPT is like adding a new recipe to your cookbook, expanding your repertoire and confidence in using this powerful tool.

***

Mastering ChatGPT Commands

As you keep interacting with ChatGPT, remember that each command is a step toward mastering this advanced AI. Whether you're using it to streamline your work, assist with studies, or satisfy your curiosity, knowing these commands is key to unlocking ChatGPT's full potential. So keep practicing, keep experimenting, and watch as what once seemed like a complex technology becomes as familiar as chatting with an old friend.

2.5 Troubleshooting Common ChatGPT Issues

You've been chatting with ChatGPT, and suddenly, it's acting up—either not responding, giving weird answers, or just going silent. Frustrating, right? Don't worry! This is your "ChatGPT First Aid" guide. Just like people, even digital tools can have off days. Let's break down how to fix these issues with some easy steps.

Connectivity Issues

First, check your internet connection. A quick test is to load a video online. If it plays smoothly, your internet is fine. If it's buffering, try restarting your router. If you're on mobile data, make sure you haven't hit your data limit. Also, check if your device is in airplane mode or has a weak signal.

Slow Responses

Slow response times can be annoying. It's usually due to connectivity issues or high server loads. Imagine everyone asking ChatGPT questions at the same time—it can get overwhelming! Be patient and try again in a few minutes. If it keeps happening, contact support to check if there's a bigger issue.

Weird or Irrelevant Replies

Sometimes, ChatGPT might give answers that don't make sense. This happens when it misinterprets your question. Try rephrasing your query or giving more context. It's like telling your GPS which Main Street you mean. If it keeps happening, reset the app or clear the cache to give ChatGPT a fresh start.

When to Seek Help

If you've tried everything and ChatGPT is still acting up, it's time to call in the experts. Most platforms have a support section. Don't hesitate to use it—they're like tech superheroes ready to help you.

Preventing Future Issues

To avoid problems, keep your software updated. Updates fix bugs and improve performance. Regularly clear your cache and cookies to keep things running smoothly. Also, make sure your device isn't overloaded with apps running in the background. A tidy workspace leads to better productivity.

With these tips, you're ready to tackle common ChatGPT issues. Troubleshoot like a pro to enjoy smooth and fun digital chats!

2.6 Enhancing Privacy and Security When Using ChatGPT

Using AI like ChatGPT is like being in an exciting movie but with more virtual adventures! However, with great power comes great responsibility—especially with your data. Let's talk about keeping your data safe while enjoying your AI journey.

Understanding Data Privacy

Whenever you chat with ChatGPT, your data—like your questions and preferences—is processed to create responses. This data can include your location, device info, and browsing history. Keeping your data private ensures your information stays personal. It's not just about secrets; it's about controlling your digital footprint.

***

Configuring Privacy Settings

Locking down your data starts with configuring privacy settings. Understand the platform's privacy policies—yes, they can be boring, but they are important! Adjust settings to limit data sharing and turn off location services if you don't need them. It's like setting up a security system for your digital home.

Safe Usage Practices

Be mindful of the information you share. Just like you wouldn't give your house keys to a stranger, don't share too much personal info with ChatGPT. Use strong, unique passwords, enable two-factor authentication, and watch out for phishing scams. These are sneaky tricks that look legit but aren't.

Legal and Ethical Considerations

Using AI responsibly is crucial, especially in sensitive areas like healthcare or finance. Ensure you follow regulations like GDPR in Europe, which protect personal data. Ethically, understand AI's limits—while ChatGPT can help, it shouldn't replace professional judgment in critical decisions.

Protecting Your Digital Interactions

By prioritizing privacy and security, you make ChatGPT a safe and helpful tool. It becomes a reliable source of information and support. So, keep your digital safety belt fastened as you explore AI—it's your best defense in this exciting journey.

With these privacy and security tips, you're ready to enjoy ChatGPT safely. Keep this guide handy—your AI adventure is just beginning, and the best is yet to come!

Chapter 2 - Exercises

Exercise 1: Interactive Chat with ChatGPT

Objective: Gain hands-on experience with ChatGPT and understand its capabilities.

Instructions:

1. Use an online platform that offers access to ChatGPT or a similar AI chatbot.
2. Ask ChatGPT the following questions:
- What is artificial intelligence?
- Can you help me write a polite email to my boss?
- What are some uses of AI in everyday life?
3. Evaluate the responses you receive. How accurate and helpful are they? Note any areas where the AI's understanding or response might have been lacking.

Tip: Check out this YouTube video about how to install and use ChatGPT on your iPhone.

Exercise 2: Platform Choices

Objective: Understand the different ways to interact with ChatGPT and the benefits of each platform.

Instructions:

1. List three different platforms through which you can interact with ChatGPT.
- Provide examples such as web-based platforms, mobile apps, or integrations within other software.
2. How can dedicated apps for ChatGPT on mobile devices improve accessibility, convenience, push notifications, and offline capabilities for users?

Exercise 3: Software Updates and User Settings

Objective: Recognize the importance of keeping ChatGPT software updated and managing user settings effectively.

Instructions:

1. What is the importance of keeping your software updated in ChatGPT? How do updates enhance security, improve performance, and provide new features?
2. List the actions you can take in your user profile settings in ChatGPT. Include examples like updating personal information, managing notification preferences, and customizing interaction settings.

Exercise 4: Effective Communication with ChatGPT

Objective: Learn how to communicate effectively with ChatGPT to get the best responses.

Instructions:

1. Create a practice exercise where you ask specific questions to ChatGPT and then explain how this improves response accuracy and relevance.

2. List the benefits of engaging in a back-and-forth dialogue with ChatGPT and highlight advantages like refined answers, deeper insights, and a more interactive experience.

Exercise 5: Personalizing ChatGPT Interactions

Objective: Understand how to personalize your ChatGPT experience for better usability.

Instructions:

1. What is the importance of adjusting the response length and complexity in the ChatGPT settings?

2. List ways in which setting up shortcuts and macros can enhance your experience with ChatGPT and provide examples like automating frequent tasks and streamlining interactions.

Exercise 6: Troubleshooting Common Issues

Objective: Learn how to identify and solve common problems when using ChatGPT.

Instructions:

1. What are some common issues that users might face when interacting with ChatGPT? Provide examples such as connectivity problems, slow responses, or misunderstood queries.

2. What are the steps to address connectivity issues when using ChatGPT?

3. What actions can users take if ChatGPT continues to deliver unexpected outputs?

Chapter Three

Practical Applications of AI and ChatGPT: Making ChatGPT Your Own

Imagine waking up to your AI assistant gently telling you your schedule for the day. Meanwhile, your coffee is being made just the way you like it. This isn't from a futuristic movie—it's your new reality with ChatGPT! Let's explore how AI, especially ChatGPT, can make your life easier and more fun. It's not just about complicated stuff; it's about adding a personal touch to your everyday life.

***

CHAPTER 3

3.1 Integrating ChatGPT in Daily Personal Tasks

Task Automation

First off, let's talk about task automation. Think of ChatGPT as your personal assistant who never forgets anything. No more missed appointments or late bill payments! ChatGPT can handle routine tasks like scheduling appointments, sending reminders, or managing your emails. It turns your to-do list into a done list. For example, you can teach ChatGPT when you prefer to have meetings or how you like your daily summary of tasks. It can automatically arrange your calendar, set reminders just for you, and even prioritize your emails. It's like having a secretary available 24/7 without needing coffee breaks.

Personal Assistant Features

ChatGPT can also be your morning newsreader, weather forecaster, and lifestyle advisor. Imagine asking, "Do I need an umbrella today?" and getting a quick response along with the day's temperature and any important weather alerts. If you want the latest stock market news or a recap of last night's game, ChatGPT has you covered. You can customize these interactions to get information based on your interests and preferences, making sure you stay updated effortlessly.

Interaction with Smart Home Devices

Now, let's add some tech! ChatGPT can work with your smart home devices. With simple voice or text commands, you can control your lights, adjust the thermostat, or even check on home security. Imagine you're snuggled in bed, and it's cold. Instead of getting up, you text ChatGPT, "Hey, can you turn up the heat to 70 degrees?" and it does. This makes your home more comfortable and energy-efficient by optimizing usage based on your habits.

Customization Tips

Lastly, let's talk about customization. Personalizing ChatGPT to fit your needs can make it even better. Start by setting up user profiles for everyone in your family. ChatGPT can learn each person's preferences, from news topics to room temperature, and interact accordingly. You can also set up voice recognition for a more seamless experience. Imagine ChatGPT recognizing your voice and switching to your personal settings instantly. Additionally, use widgets or shortcuts for commands you use often. A single tap could give you traffic updates, turn on your home security system, or start your coffee maker.

By integrating ChatGPT into your daily routines, you're not just using a tool—you're adopting a lifestyle where technology and convenience meet. Whether it's through automating tasks, staying updated easily, controlling your home environment, or customizing interactions, ChatGPT is here to make your life better. Why wait for the future when you can live it today? Let ChatGPT be your assistant, home manager, and daily planner, all in one.

3.2 Using AI for Enhanced Content Creation

Let's say you have a blog that's always hungry for new posts or a social media feed that's been quiet for too long. AI is your new creative helper, making content creation super easy. You might wonder, "Can a bunch of circuits and code really help me write?" Absolutely, and here's how it's changing the game for creators everywhere.

AI tools like Jasper and Writesonic are more than just producing robotic texts. They are about crafting stories, inspiring ideas, and making sure your grammar is perfect. These tools are like brainstorming with a team of writers, each helping to shape your narrative. You start by giving a topic or a headline, and they generate a draft quickly. Need a blog post about the best coffee shops in your city? Or catchy captions for Instagram? Just try these tools, and they will create relevant and engaging content.

But here's the exciting part. AI doesn't just generate content; it boosts your creativity. Ever felt stuck with a boring tone or style? AI can suggest variations, pushing your creative boundaries. It's like playing a video game where you can switch characters anytime. One minute, you're writing like a witty columnist, and the next, you're exploring a poetic style. These AI-generated suggestions are based on learning from various writing styles and genres, giving you options you might not have considered.

Interactive Writing Prompts

To get your creative juices flowing, why not try an interactive exercise? Here's a fun challenge:

1. Pick a topic you love and input it into an AI writing tool.

2. Set the style to something you've never tried—maybe a humorous take if you're usually more serious or a poetic style if you're typically straightforward.

3. See how the AI transforms your idea and take it as a starting point to explore new dimensions in your writing.

It's like creative cross-training; you'll become more versatile and inspired!

Now, onto editing and proofreading. AI here is like having a vigilant proofreader who never sleeps. Tools like Grammarly or Hemingway don't just catch typos; they help refine your sentences, making your writing crisp and clear. Imagine these tools as the friendly grammar experts looking over your shoulder, suggesting better ways to phrase your thoughts, and ensuring your writing is correct and compelling.

Of course, with great power comes great responsibility—especially with authenticity and ethics in AI-assisted content creation. While AI can generate content based on the data it's trained on, keeping the human touch is crucial. You're the captain; AI is just the navigation tool. Make sure the content reflects your unique voice and ethical standards. It's tempting to accept every AI suggestion, but it's important to vet these and keep your content genuine and true to your values. Authenticity connects deeply with readers, and maintaining that trust is key.

By embracing AI in content creation, you're not just keeping up with the times; you're stepping into a role where technology lifts you beyond the mundane, freeing you up for the creative and enjoyable aspects of content crafting. Whether generating fresh posts, sprucing up your style, or polishing your prose, AI makes every word count. Get ready to transform your content from good to great with AI's help. In the digital age, being a content creator isn't just about writing; it's about being creatively limitless.

3.3 Managing Money With AI

Let's talk about something that affects everyone: money. Managing finances sometimes feels like trying to nail jelly to the wall, right? But what if I told you that AI could make it as easy as pie? No more guesswork, no more forgotten bills, and no more "Oops, I overspent on coffee this month." AI is here to transform financial management from a dreaded chore into a streamlined, almost enjoyable task.

Budgeting and Expense Tracking

First up, let's dive into budgeting and expense tracking. Remember the old days of scribbling expenses in a notebook or typing them into a massive, confusing spreadsheet? Well, AI bids farewell to all that hassle. Modern AI-powered finance apps can automatically track your spending, categorize expenses, and even analyze your financial habits to offer personalized budgeting advice. Imagine an app that notices you spend a lot on eating out and suggests budget adjustments or finds you better deals. This isn't just about tracking; it's about optimizing your spending to fit your lifestyle and financial goals. These apps use algorithms to forecast your future financial scenario based on current trends in your spending, giving you a clear vision of where you might be heading financially. It's like having an economic crystal ball powered by AI, ensuring you can plan for that holiday or big purchase without stress.

***

Investment Insights

Next, let's talk about investments. AI is your savvy guide if the stock market has always seemed like a wild jungle of unpredictability. AI tools in investment platforms analyze vast amounts of market data to provide insights and predictions that were previously only accessible to professional traders. These tools study patterns in market data to forecast trends and can alert you about the best times to buy or sell stocks. They make sense of complex financial news and global economic indicators in real time, giving you a digest that's easy to understand. For instance, if you're pondering whether to invest in tech stocks or green energy, AI can provide data-driven insights based on historical performance, market conditions, and future industry projections. This way, you're not just guessing; you're making informed decisions that maximize your potential returns.

Fraud Detection

On to a critical aspect of financial management—security. Financial fraud can be a nightmare in an age where digital transactions are the norm. Here's where AI steps in as your financial watchdog. AI-powered fraud detection systems like Kount and Sift actively monitor your transaction history to swiftly identify any irregularities in your activity. If there's a transaction from a country you've never shopped from or a sudden large amount charged to your account, AI flags it immediately. It's like having a highly attentive bodyguard for your finances, always looking for anything fishy. These systems learn from thousands of fraud cases, making them adept at sniffing out even the most cunning fraud attempts, ensuring your money's safety.

Let's say you typically make purchases within your country and have a consistent spending pattern. One day, a transaction is initiated from a different country using your account details, or a large sum of money is charged to your account out of the blue. An AI-powered fraud detection system immediately recognizes this as unusual activity based on your transaction history and flags it for review. This quick detection helps prevent potential financial fraud and protects your assets.

***

Financial Planning Tools

Finally, let's explore AI-driven financial planning tools. Planning your financial future can be daunting, but AI makes it accessible and straightforward. These tools help you set and track financial goals, whether saving for retirement, buying a home, or setting up a college fund. They analyze your financial data, suggest how much you need to save each month, and even adjust your plan based on changes in your income or expenses. It's like having a personal financial advisor in your pocket, available 24/7 to guide you through the maze of financial planning. This way, you're saving money and strategically planning for a financially secure future aligned with your dreams.

One way to integrate AI into your personal finance management is by using AI-powered apps like Wally, Cleo, and Rocket Money. These apps can analyze your spending habits, provide tailored budgeting advice, and offer insights into investment opportunities. They can also help you track your expenses, set financial goals, and provide personalized recommendations to improve your financial health. By leveraging AI technology, these apps can simplify managing your finances and help you make more informed decisions, ultimately empowering you to take control of your financial well-being.

3.4 ChatGPT for Learning

Let's flip the classroom script and meet your new favorite study buddy, ChatGPT. Forget cramming from textbooks the night before an exam. With ChatGPT, you've got a tutoring genius ready to help anytime. Stuck on a physics problem? Ask ChatGPT. Need help with a Shakespeare essay? ChatGPT's got you covered. It's like having a mini-Einstein in your pocket, turning tough homework into "Aha!" moments.

Language Learning

Now, let's spice things up with language learning. Learning a new language is more than memorizing words; it's about conversation, context, and culture. ChatGPT can be your interactive language partner, engaging in dialogues that go beyond rote repetition. Whether chatting in French or tackling Mandarin, ChatGPT can simulate real-life conversations and provide instant feedback on grammar and pronunciation. It's like having a language coach always ready for a chat, helping you practice until new words and phrases stick.

Research Assistance

For research, ChatGPT is like a personal assistant. Instead of combing through tons of articles, books, and journals, let ChatGPT help. It can quickly find relevant facts, summarize papers, or generate citations. Whether you're a high school student on your first big project or a grad student deep in thesis work, ChatGPT makes research faster and more efficient.

Interactive Learning

ChatGPT can also make learning interactive and fun. Imagine learning about the solar system not just from a textbook but through a simulation where you explore each planet. ChatGPT can guide you through educational games, role-playing scenarios, or problem-solving adventures, making learning active and enjoyable. It's like bringing joy back to education, replacing boring lectures with dynamic interactions that spark curiosity and understanding.

Personalized Learning

ChatGPT understands everyone learns differently. Whether you like learning through images and videos or hands-on activities, ChatGPT adapts to your style, ensuring your educational journey is tailored to you.

Integrating ChatGPT into education isn't just about convenience; it's about transforming how we learn. From personalized tutoring and language practice to efficient research and interactive learning, ChatGPT makes learning more accessible and fun. Whether mastering a new skill, preparing for an exam, or just curious, let ChatGPT turn every challenge into a chance to learn and grow.

***

3.5 Organizing Your Life with AI

Imagine your life as a busy city. AI is like the best city planner, helping you navigate everything smoothly. AI can juggle your personal and professional life, making sure everything runs well.

Smart Scheduling

Starting with your calendar, AI doesn't just remind you about appointments. It integrates into your schedule, knowing your workflow and preferences. For example, if you have a meeting at 2 PM and a doctor's appointment at 4 PM, AI might suggest lunch with a client in between to save time. AI ensures you're never double-booked and have enough breaks, keeping your day running smoothly.

Task Prioritization

AI also helps prioritize tasks. It sorts your to-do list based on urgency and personal preferences. For example, AI might suggest finishing a report due tomorrow before planning a party next week. It helps you work smarter, not harder, by figuring out what to do next.

Smart Reminders

AI's reminder systems are like having a personal coach. It sends reminders at the right time and in a way that fits your day. For instance, if you have a presentation, AI might remind you a week in advance to start preparing and check in periodically to see your progress. It ensures you're always on top of tasks, like paying bills or preparing for meetings.

App Integration

AI can also integrate with other apps for seamless organization. For example, AI can link to your email, project management tools, fitness tracker, and social media. It can scan emails for travel plans, update your calendar, remind you to check in for flights, and suggest the best times to post on social media. AI ensures everything in your digital life works together.

Organizing your life with AI turns chaos into a well-oiled machine. From managing your calendar and prioritizing tasks to setting smart reminders and integrating with other apps, AI makes life smoother and more efficient. Let AI take the wheel and watch as it transforms your daily chaos into a calm, well-planned, and enjoyable journey.

3.6 Creative Writing with AI: Composing Poetry and Stories

Have you ever stared at a blank page, waiting for inspiration to strike like a lightning bolt from a clear sky? Enter AI, your new creative partner in crime, turning the daunting white space into a playground of words and ideas. Let's peel back the curtain on how AI is not just a tool but a collaborator in creative writing, whether you're penning down a sonnet or spinning a yarn for your next short story. When it comes to sparking creativity, AI is like that friend who always has a quirky idea up their sleeve.

Imagine you're trying to write a piece about a city you've never visited. You could spend hours trawling through travel blogs or ask your AI buddy to generate a setting based on its vast database of world knowledge. With a few clicks, you receive a vivid description of bustling streets, aromatic food stalls, and the distant hum of nightlife—all rich details that can set the scene for your narrative. It's like having a muse on demand, providing you with creative writing prompts, story ideas, or poetic lines that capture the essence of the emotion or scene you're trying to convey. This spark of inspiration is invaluable, especially when writer's block looms like an unwelcome shadow over your creative process.

Let's transition from muse to co-writer, where AI's capabilities extend into drafting and developing narratives. Envision: you're crafting a complex story with multiple characters, each with intricate backstories and interconnected fates. AI can jazz up your story by tossing ideas to keep the plot juicy and your readers' attention glued. It's like having a writing BFF who can suggest killer dialogue that fits each character perfectly and recommend plot twists to keep things super interesting. AI amps up your storytelling game, adding a fresh spin you might not have thought of before. Finishing this analogy laundry list, AI is like brainstorming with a partner who's read every book in the library and can switch between genres and styles at the drop of a hat.

Speaking of styles, have you ever wanted to write like Shakespeare? Or channel the sparse style of Hemingway. Here's where AI really flexes its linguistic muscles. Through style mimicry, AI tools analyze and replicate the stylistic elements of other writers, offering you a palette of writing styles with which to experiment. This isn't just about copying—it's about learning and integrating diverse writing techniques into your own unique narrative voice. Whether you're looking to explore new horizons in poetic diction or want to master the art of minimalistic prose, AI can guide you through these stylistic nuances, making your journey into different literary styles both educational and thrilling.

Now, let's touch on the editing phase—often less glamorous but equally crucial. AI comes equipped with tools that provide immediate feedback on your creative drafts. Think of it as having an editor on call, ready to suggest enhancements or spot inconsistencies. Whether it's tightening up your prose, improving the flow of a poem, or just catching those pesky typos, AI's feedback is invaluable for refining your work. This real-time critique polishes your writing and accelerates your writing growth by providing consistent, constructive feedback. For example, if you're working on a short story, AI can point out areas where the plot may be unclear or where the character development needs more depth.

Harnessing AI in your creative writing process opens up a world where the boundaries of creativity are continually expanded and redefined. Imagine you're crafting a fantasy novel and need inspiration for a magical kingdom. AI can generate detailed descriptions of landscapes, suggest unique character traits, or even create snippets of dialogue, providing the initial spark of inspiration. From the initial spark to the final touches of revision, AI supports and enhances your creative endeavors, making the journey from an idea to a fully realized piece of writing smoother and more enjoyable. So, the next time you face the daunting white space, remember that AI is your ally, ready to fill it with your imagination's vibrant, vivid, and varied hues.

As we finish looking at how AI is used in creative writing, it's clear that combining technology and art can be very powerful and transformative. AI is not here to replace the human touch in literature but to enrich it, to make it more accessible, and to inspire writers to push the boundaries of their creativity. Whether you're a novice poet or a seasoned novelist, AI has something to offer at every stage of your writing process, from the moment of inspiration to the final draft.

Looking ahead, the next chapter will delve into how AI is reshaping industries beyond the literary world. From healthcare to finance, we'll explore the groundbreaking ways in which AI is not just a tool but a catalyst for innovation, driving changes and reshaping our world. Stay tuned because the best is yet to come, and with AI by your side, every exploration is an opportunity for discovery.

3.7 Creating Images with AI: A Beginner's Guide

Imagine you have a picture in your mind—a beautiful sunset over the ocean, a futuristic city, or even a dragon flying through the sky. Now, imagine being able to bring that picture to life, just like magic! With AI, creating images from your imagination is easier than ever, even if you're a beginner. Let's dive into how you can start making your own digital masterpieces with the help of AI.

What is AI Image Generation?

AI image generation is like having an artist in your computer. You tell it what you want—like a blue dragon or a pink sky—and the AI creates an image based on your description. It's as if the computer reads your mind and then paints what you're thinking about!

Understanding DALL-E: Your AI Art Partner

One of the most popular tools for AI image generation is DALL-E. Created by OpenAI, DALL-E is designed to turn your text descriptions into stunning images. It combines creativity and technology, allowing you to create everything from realistic scenes to fantastical worlds.

DALL-E is great for beginners because it's easy to use and delivers instant results. Whether you describe "a cozy cottage in a snowy forest" or "a cat wearing a hat in space," DALL-E can bring your vision to life in seconds. The more detailed and specific your description, the more accurately DALL-E can create the image you imagine.

How to Get Started

1. **Choose the Right Tool:**
    - To start creating images with AI, you'll need a special tool. As mentioned, DALL-E is an excellent choice, but other options like . These tools are

designed to be user-friendly, even if you've never done anything like this before.

- Midjourney

- and

- Stable Diffusion exist

2. **Write a Description:**

    - Once your tool is ready, the next step is to describe what you want to create. For example, if you want to see a magical forest, you might type, "A forest with glowing trees and a sparkling river under a full moon." The more detailed your description, the more the AI will understand what you want.

3. **Generate Your Image:**

    - After you've typed your description, you simply click a button, and the AI goes to work. You'll have an image that matches your description in just a few seconds. It's like watching a painting come to life right before your eyes!

4. **Experiment and Have Fun:**

    - Don't worry if your first image isn't exactly what you imagined. You can always tweak your description or try new ideas. The more you play around, the better you'll get at guiding the AI to create exactly what you want.

Tips for Success

- **Be Specific:** The more details you provide in your description, the more accurate your image will be. Instead of saying "a tree," you might say "a tall oak tree with golden leaves."

- **Use Imagination:** Don't be afraid to get creative! AI can create almost anything you can think of, so let your imagination run wild.

- **Practice Makes Perfect:** The more you practice, the better you'll become at using AI to create stunning images. Keep experimenting with different ideas and descriptions.

Why It's Awesome

Creating images with AI is not only fun, but it also helps you express your creativity in new ways. Whether you want to design a cool background for your phone, create characters for a story, or just play around with different ideas, AI image generation is a powerful tool that can bring your imagination to life.

So, why not give it a try? With just a few clicks, you can start creating your own digital art—no paintbrush is required!

3.8 AI in Video Creation and Editing

AI Video Editing: Imagine editing videos like a pro without spending hours on it. AI tools like Adobe Sensei help you do things like color correction and adding cool transitions automatically. You just describe what you want, like "make this scene brighter," and the AI does it for you. This makes creating videos for school projects, YouTube, or social media super easy.

Automatic Video Making: Tools like Pictory and Synthesia let you create videos just by typing out a script. For example, you can write a short story or a news report, and the AI will turn it into a video with animations and voiceovers. This is perfect for creating quick videos without needing a camera or fancy equipment.

3.9 AI in Music and Sound Creation

AI-Made Music: Ever wanted to create your own music but didn't know how? AI tools like AIVA let you compose music by picking a genre or mood. You can make a soundtrack for a video game, a podcast, or just for fun, even if you've never played an instrument before.

Sound Editing: AI tools like Descript make editing audio as easy as editing text. For example, if you make a podcast, you can cut out mistakes just by deleting words from the transcript. AI can also help you add sound effects, making your audio projects sound professional.

3.10 AI in Personal Health and Fitness

AI Fitness Coach: Apps like Freeletics use AI to create workout plans just for you. The AI learns what exercises work best for you and changes your workout routine as you get stronger. It's like having a personal trainer in your pocket!

Mental Health Support: AI tools like Woebot chat with you to help manage stress and anxiety. They can guide you through exercises that make you feel better and check in on how you're doing. It's a bit like having a friendly counselor who's always there when you need to talk.

3.11 AI in Shopping and Fashion

Shopping is changing fast, especially with the rise of online shopping. AI shopping assistants are helping to make the experience better and more personal for everyone. They use technology to help shoppers find what they want more easily. Here are some key facts about how these assistants work and their importance. Read more at: https://masterofcode.com/blog/personal-shopper-app

Key Facts:

1. **Future of Shopping** – By 2040, most people (95%) will shop online.

2. **Growth of Online Business** – The online business market is expected to grow quickly, by almost 19% each year until 2028.

3. **What AI Shopping Assistants Do** – AI shopping assistants help people find products they want and make shopping easier and more personal.

4. **Why Personalization Matters** – Most shoppers (86%) want personalized experiences, and 45% are more likely to buy from places that offer tailored suggestions.

5. **Using Chatbots** – Chatbots are computer programs that help customers by answering questions anytime, making shopping better.

6. **Cool Shopping Apps** – Apps like H&M's and eBags let users find items using pictures and track what's available in stores.

7. **Voice Assistants** – Voice assistants can help people find products, check prices, and even place orders using voice commands.

3.12 AI in Smart Assistants and Voice Technology

Voice Cloning: Imagine creating a voice that sounds just like you—or even a famous person! Tools like Resemble AI can create a realistic copy of your voice. This can be used for fun projects like making custom voice assistants or recording stories in your voice.

Smart Chatbots: AI chatbots like those used by companies can answer questions and help with customer service. They can chat with you just like a real person, helping you find what you need quickly. This makes shopping or getting help online faster and easier.

3.13 AI in Education and Learning

Personalized Learning: AI tools like Knewton help make learning easier by adjusting to how well you understand the material. If you're struggling with a math problem, AI gives you more practice on that topic. It's like having a tutor who knows exactly what you need to work on.

AI Language Learning: Apps like Duolingo use AI to help you learn a new language at your own pace. The AI adjusts lessons based on what you've mastered and what you still need to practice. It also lets you practice real-life conversations, making it easier to learn how to speak a new language.

***

Chapter 3 Exercises: Practical Applications of AI and ChatGPT

Exercise 1: Integrating ChatGPT in Daily Personal Tasks

Objective: Explore how ChatGPT can automate and simplify daily personal tasks.
   Instructions:

PRACTICAL APPLICATIONS OF AI AND CHATGPT: MAKING... 45

1. **Task Automation**:
    - List three tasks you would like to automate using ChatGPT (e.g., scheduling appointments, sending reminders, managing emails).
    - Describe how ChatGPT can help automate each task and the benefits of doing so.

2. **Personal Assistant Features**:
    - Identify three types of information you would like ChatGPT to provide daily (e.g., weather updates, news summaries, stock market news).
    - Explain how receiving this information from ChatGPT can enhance your daily routine.

3. **Interaction with Smart Home Devices**:
    - List three smart home devices you have or plan to use.
    - Describe how integrating ChatGPT with these devices can improve convenience and energy efficiency in your home.

4. **Customization Tips:**
    - List three customization options for ChatGPT that would enhance your user experience (e.g., setting up user profiles, voice recognition, and widgets).
    - Explain how each customization option can make your interactions with ChatGPT more personalized and efficient.

Exercise 2: Using AI for Enhanced Content Creation

Objective: Understand how AI can assist in generating and refining content for various platforms.

Instructions:

1. **AI Tools for Content Creation**:
    - List three AI tools to help create content (e.g., Jasper, Writesonic, Grammarly).
    - Describe the main features of each tool and how they can aid in your content creation process.

2. **Interactive Writing Prompts**:
   - Choose a topic you enjoy and input it into an AI writing tool.
   - Set the style to something new for you (e.g., humorous, poetic) and describe how the AI transformed your idea.
   - Reflect on how this exercise helped expand your writing style.

3. **Editing and Proofreading:**
   - Use an AI tool like Grammarly or Hemingway to edit your writing.
   - List the leading corrections or suggestions provided by the AI.
   - Explain how these suggestions improved your writing.

4. **Ethical Considerations:**
   - Discuss the importance of maintaining authenticity when using AI for content creation.
   - List two ways to ensure the content remains genuine and reflects your unique voice.

Exercise 3: AI in Managing Personal Finances

Objective: Explore how AI can help manage personal finances efficiently.

Instructions:

1. **Budgeting and Expense Tracking**:
   - Identify three AI-powered finance apps that help with budgeting and expense tracking.
   - Describe how each app can optimize spending and provide personalized budgeting advice.

2. **Investment Insights**:
   - Choose an AI tool that provides investment insights.
   - Explain how this tool analyzes market data and helps you make informed investment decisions.

PRACTICAL APPLICATIONS OF AI AND CHATGPT: MAKING... 47

3. **Fraud Detection**:
   - List three ways AI can help detect and prevent financial fraud.
   - Describe a scenario where AI successfully prevented a fraudulent transaction.

4. **Financial Planning Tools**:
   - Identify an AI-driven financial planning tool.
   - Discuss how this tool can help you set and track financial goals.

Exercise 4: ChatGPT for Educational Support and Learning

Objective: Utilize ChatGPT as an educational tool for enhanced learning.

Instructions:

1. **Personalized Tutoring**:
   - Choose a challenging subject and ask ChatGPT to explain a specific concept.
   - Describe how ChatGPT's explanation helped clarify the concept.

2. **Language Learning**:
   - Engage in a conversation with ChatGPT in a language you are learning.
   - List three ways this interaction improved your language skills (e.g., grammar, vocabulary, pronunciation).

3. **Research Assistance**:
   - Use ChatGPT to help with a research project.
   - Describe how ChatGPT assisted in gathering information, summarizing research papers, or generating citations.

4. **Interactive Learning**:
   - Identify an interactive learning scenario where ChatGPT can assist (e.g., exploring the solar system or solving math problems).
   - Explain how this interactive approach made learning more engaging and effective.

Exercise 5: Organizing Your Life with AI

Objective: Learn how AI can help organize and manage personal and professional tasks efficiently.

Instructions:

1. **Calendar Management:**
   - Describe how AI can help manage your calendar and optimize your schedule.
   - List three benefits of using AI for calendar management.

2. **Task Prioritization:**
   - Identify three tasks from your to-do list and explain how AI can help prioritize them.
   - Describe the impact of AI-assisted task prioritization on your productivity.

3. **Smart Reminders:**
   - Set up reminders for three important tasks using an AI tool.
   - Explain how AI ensures timely and effective reminders.

4. **Integration with Other Apps:**
   - Choose three apps you use regularly and describe how integrating them with AI can streamline your workflow.
   - Explain the benefits of having a connected and synchronized digital environment.

Exercise 6: Creative Writing with AI

Objective: Enhance creative writing skills using AI tools.

Instructions:

1. **Generating Ideas:**
   - Use AI to generate ideas for a new story or poem.
   - Describe the ideas generated and how they inspired your writing.

2. Drafting and Development:

- Write a draft of a story or poem using AI suggestions.

- Explain how AI's input influenced the development of your narrative or poem.

3. Style Mimicry:

- Choose a literary style you admire and ask AI to help mimic that style in your writing.

- Describe how AI-assisted style mimicry expanded your writing techniques.

4. Editing and Feedback:

- Use AI tools to edit your writing and receive feedback.

- List the main improvements suggested by the AI and explain how they enhanced your work.

Exercise 7: Creating Your First AI-Generated Image

Objective: Learn how to create a digital image using AI by practicing with a simple and fun task.

Instructions:

1. Choose Your AI Tool:

- Pick an AI image-generation tool like **DALL-E**, **Midjourney**, or **Stable Diffusion**. If you're not sure where to start, look up one of these tools online and sign up for an account.

2. Write a Description:

- Think of a simple image you'd like to create. It could be anything—a rainbow over a field, a futuristic robot, or a castle in the clouds. Write a short, clear description of the image you want to see.

- Example: "A cozy cottage in a snowy forest with smoke coming from the chimney."

3. Generate Your Image:
- Use your chosen AI tool to create the image based on your description. Follow the steps provided by the tool to input your description and generate the image.

4. Experiment with Variations:
- After seeing your first image, try making some changes to your description. Add more details or change something about the scene.
- Example: "A cozy cottage in a snowy forest at sunset with a deer standing nearby."
- Generate a new image with the updated description.

5. Reflect on Your Creation:
- Look at the images you've created and think about what you liked or what surprised you. Did the AI capture what you imagined? How did changing the description affect the image?
- Write a few sentences about your experience and what you learned from creating your images.

6. Share Your Work (Optional):
- If you're proud of your creations, consider sharing them with friends, family, or online communities. See what others think of your AI-generated artwork!

Exercise 8: AI in Video Creation and Editing

Exercise: Create a Simple Video

- **Objective:** Learn how to use AI to create and edit a short video.
- **Instructions:**

    a. Choose an AI video tool like **Pictory** or **Synthesia**.

    b. Write a short script (2-3 sentences) about a topic you like (e.g., "Why I love pizza").

    c. Use the AI tool to turn your script into a video. Add animations or voiceovers if available.

d. Experiment with editing features like adding transitions or adjusting colors.

e. Watch your video and share it with a friend or family member.

Exercise 9: AI in Music and Sound Creation

Exercise: Compose Your Own Music

- **Objective:** Create a short piece of music using AI.
- **Instructions:**

    a. Choose an AI music tool like **AIVA** or **Amper Music**.

    b. Pick a genre (e.g., rock, classical, or pop) and a mood (e.g., happy, calm).

    c. Let the AI generate a short piece of music (30 seconds to 1 minute).

    d. Listen to the music and think about where you could use it (e.g., background music for a video).

    e. If possible, adjust the instruments or tempo to see how it changes the feel of the music.

Exercise 10: AI in Personal Health and Fitness

Exercise: Start a Personalized Workout Plan

- **Objective:** Use AI to create a workout plan that fits your needs.
- **Instructions:**

    a. Download an AI fitness app like **Freeletics** or **FitnessAI**.

    b. Enter your fitness goals (e.g., getting stronger, losing weight).

    c. Follow the workout plan suggested by the AI for a week.

d. Note how the AI adjusts the exercises based on your progress.

e. Reflect on how the AI's suggestions helped you improve your fitness routine.

Exercise 11: AI in Shopping and Fashion

Exercise: Discover Your Style with AI

- **Objective:** Use AI to find clothing or accessories that match your style.

- **Instructions:**

    a. Try a fashion AI tool like **The Yes**.

    b. Browse through a few items and rate them (like or dislike) to help the AI learn your preferences.

    c. Let the AI suggest outfits or accessories based on your ratings.

    d. Pick one outfit or item that you like the most.

    e. Imagine how you would wear it or pair it with other clothes you own.

Exercise 12: AI in Smart Assistants and Voice Technology

Exercise: Create a Custom Voice Assistant

- **Objective:** Use AI to make a simple voice assistant that responds in a custom voice.

- **Instructions:**

    a. Choose an AI voice tool like **Resemble AI**.

    b. Record a short sample of your voice (e.g., "Hello, how can I help you?").

    c. Use the AI to create a voice clone.

    d. Set up the voice assistant to respond to simple commands (e.g., asking for

PRACTICAL APPLICATIONS OF AI AND CHATGPT: MAKING...

the weather).

e. Test your voice assistant by asking it a few questions.

Exercise 13: AI in Education and Learning

Exercise: Personalized Learning with AI

- **Objective:** Use AI to improve your skills in a subject you're studying.

- **Instructions:**

    a. Pick a subject you want to improve in (e.g., math, history).

    b. Use an AI learning platform like **Knewton** or a language app like **Duolingo**.

    c. Complete a lesson or activity.

    d. Let the AI give you feedback or suggest what to study next.

    e. Reflect on how the AI's suggestions helped you understand the subject better.

Outcome Section: Chapter 3 Exercises

By completing these exercises, you have gained hands-on experience in various practical applications of AI and ChatGPT. Each exercise was designed to introduce you to different AI tools and techniques, helping you to integrate AI into your daily life, creative projects, personal finance management, health routines, and learning processes.

Key Outcomes:

1. **Enhanced Daily Efficiency:** You've learned how ChatGPT and other AI tools can automate and streamline everyday tasks, making your life more organized and productive. From managing schedules to creating reminders, AI can now assist you in keeping your day running smoothly.

2. **Creative Empowerment:** Through exercises in content creation, video editing, music composition, and image generation, you've explored how AI can boost

your creativity. Whether generating new ideas or refining your work, AI has shown you new ways to express your creativity with ease and innovation.

3. **Improved Financial Management:** With the help of AI-powered finance apps, you now have the tools to better manage your budget, make informed investment decisions, and protect yourself from financial fraud. AI has simplified the complex world of personal finance, making it more accessible and manageable.

4. **Health and Fitness Optimization:** By integrating AI into your health and fitness routines, you've learned how to personalize workout plans and support your mental well-being. AI has become your virtual coach, helping you achieve your health goals with tailored advice and support.

5. **Personalized Shopping Experience:** AI has introduced you to a more personalized shopping experience where you can discover clothing and accessories that match your style. You've seen how AI can help you make better shopping choices, all from the comfort of your home.

6. **Advanced Learning and Education:** Through personalized learning experiences with AI, you've enhanced your understanding of various subjects. AI tools have provided you with targeted feedback, making your learning journey more effective and enjoyable.

7. **Technological Confidence:** These exercises have helped build your confidence in using AI tools and technology. You now have a better understanding of how AI can be a powerful ally in various aspects of life, from creative endeavors to personal development.

By exploring these AI trends and completing the exercises, you are now equipped with the knowledge and skills to continue integrating AI into your life. Whether for personal growth, creative projects, or everyday convenience, AI is here to help you achieve more and make your life easier and more enjoyable.

Chapter Four

AI in the Professional Sphere

CHAPTER 4

Ever felt like your office routine was a never-ending loop of Groundhog Day, except with more spreadsheets and less Bill Murray? Well, you're not alone, and guess what? AI is here to break the cycle. Imagine handing over those repetitive, time-consuming tasks to an AI system that does them faster, without coffee breaks, and without ever asking for a day off. This chapter is about turning your Office into a high-efficiency powerhouse with AI help. So, buckle up as we dive into the exciting world of automating routine tasks.

Who knows, perhaps you'll finally have enough free time to start that hobby you've been putting off!

***

4.1 Automating Routine Tasks with AI in the Office

Identifying Automatable Tasks

First things first: identifying what to automate. Look around your Office (or home office, as the case may be). See those tasks that are as monotonous as watching paint dry? Those are your prime candidates. We're talking about data entry, where your only challenge is not zoning out as you type; scheduling, finding a meeting time that suits everyone feels like negotiating world peace; and report generation, which often involves more copy-pasting than a high school term paper.

Here's a pro tip: start by listing well-defined and rule-based tasks—these are typically ripe for AI intervention. Think of functions where you say, "If this happens, then I do that." AI loves that kind of logic. It's like teaching a very obedient robot to bake; as long as the recipe is straightforward (and nobody throws a surprise ingredient into the mix), you're guaranteed a perfect cake every time.

Implementing Automation Tools

Now, onto the fun part: bringing in the AI muscle. Choosing the right AI tools is crucial and can be as daunting as picking a movie on a Saturday night. You want something that fits your needs, integrates seamlessly with your existing systems, and, importantly, is user-friendly—because nobody has time for a tool that needs a two-hour tutorial.

Look for AI solutions that can integrate with the software you already use. Many AI tools today come with plug-and-play functionality designed for non-techies. They can sync with your existing databases, email systems, and calendars without causing a digital meltdown. It's about enhancing what you already have, not bulldozing over your current setup.

Monitoring and Optimization

Have you got your AI tools in place? Great! But don't just set it and forget it. It's important to keep an eye on things and make improvements to use AI successfully. It's like tuning a guitar; you must keep adjusting until you hit the right notes. Keep an eye on how your AI tools are performing. Are they saving you time? Are they reducing errors? Use metrics and feedback to gauge their impact and tweak settings to meet your business needs. Think of it as having a dialogue with your AI solutions—they might not speak, but they provide plenty of data that can help you help them perform better.

Monitoring and Optimization AI Tools You Can Use:

1. Google Analytics Solutions: This tool helps you keep track of web traffic and user behavior. It shows you how well your AI-driven marketing strategies are working.

2. Hootsuite Insights: Use this tool to monitor social media engagement and see how people feel about your AI-driven content.

3. IBM Watson Studio: This platform is great for data scientists. It helps build, train, and deploy machine learning models and has strong monitoring tools.

4. Datadog: This platform monitors and provides security for cloud applications, giving real-time data and performance metrics to keep your AI systems running smoothly.

5. Splunk: This tool analyzes machine data, offering powerful analytics and insights to help you troubleshoot and optimize your AI applications.

Impact on Productivity

Here's the cool part: AI can really boost your productivity. It's not just about staying trendy with tech; it's about real benefits. AI can save you tons of time on tasks like data entry and report generation. Imagine an office where data is processed instantly, reports are ready with a click, and scheduling conflicts are super rare. That's AI at work.

For example, a medium-sized tech company used AI for customer service reports. The AI system organized and analyzed customer feedback quickly. What used to take a team a week now takes less than a day. This meant faster responses to customer issues, more time for the team to solve complex problems and higher customer satisfaction.

By automating boring tasks, AI changes office culture. It shifts focus from mundane work to strategic, creative projects. Teams become more dynamic, innovation thrives, and job satisfaction goes up. Who wouldn't be happier spending less time on spreadsheets and more on meaningful work?

Integrating AI isn't about replacing people; it's about enhancing their work. It frees up time and resources so you can focus on creativity and business growth. Embrace AI as your productivity partner, and watch it transform your daily routine into a smoother, more efficient process. Ready to give it a try? Your future self will thank you.

4.2 AI Tools for Data Analysis and Decision Making

Ever watched movies where the hero analyzes tons of data in seconds to make amazing decisions? That's not just Hollywood magic; it's real with AI-driven analytics tools. These tools are like having a super-smart, super-fast data expert on your team. They can turn mountains of data into useful insights faster than you can say "big data."

So, what are these AI-driven analytics tools? Think of them as advanced data processors that analyze large volumes of data quickly and accurately. For example, if you run an online store, an AI tool can analyze your sales data, customer feedback, and market trends all at once. It can tell you which products are popular and which are not and even predict future trends. It's like having a crystal ball powered by data.

Integrating these AI tools with your current business systems is like putting turbochargers on your car. Suddenly, you're not just collecting data; you're using it to make smarter, faster decisions. These AI tools can sync with your current systems, pulling data from various sources, analyzing it in real-time, and providing insights when needed. This helps different departments in your company work together, from marketing to sales to customer service.

With AI, you can make decisions in real-time. Traditional methods take so long to gather and analyze data that it becomes outdated. But AI tools analyze data as it comes in, allowing you to make instant decisions. For example, a stock trader can use AI tools to monitor market conditions and make buy or sell decisions quickly.

Here are some real-world examples. A large retail chain uses AI tools for inventory management. The AI system analyzed sales data and predicted product demand, optimizing inventory and saving millions in costs. Another example is a healthcare provider using AI to analyze patient data, predict high-risk patients, suggest treatments, improve patient outcomes, and reduce costs.

These stories show the power of AI in decision-making. By using AI tools, businesses can operate more dynamically, adapt quickly to market changes, and make smarter decisions. Whether optimizing operations, improving customer satisfaction, or saving costs, AI-driven data analysis tools are game-changers. Think of AI not just as an upgrade to your systems but as a key player in your strategic decision-making process. With AI, you're leading a more innovative, faster, and more informed business.

4.3 Enhancing Customer Service with ChatGPT

Imagine a world where every customer service interaction is smooth and pleasant. This isn't a fantasy; it's becoming real with AI tools like ChatGPT. Let's see how ChatGPT can transform customer service, providing consistent support and making the customer experience amazing.

Traditional customer service often involves long wait times and frustration. Enter ChatGPT, an AI-powered agent that's always ready, quick to respond, and never has a bad day. ChatGPT can handle inquiries, resolve issues, and provide information efficiently. It understands and processes natural language, making interactions feel personal and professional. It's like having a super-agent that can scale up during busy times or step in when human agents are overwhelmed. The result? Faster responses, less waiting, and happier customers.

To start using ChatGPT, integrate it into your current customer service system. It might sound tricky, but it's easier than assembling flat-pack furniture. Many AI chatbots are designed to work smoothly with common Customer Relationship Management (CRM) systems like Salesforce, HubSpot, or Drift. This integration lets ChatGPT access relevant customer data, understand the context of inquiries, and provide accurate, personalized responses. It's about creating a seamless connection between your AI tools and CRM systems, ensuring data flows smoothly, and empowering ChatGPT to deliver top-notch service.

Personalization is where AI shines. By tapping into customer data, ChatGPT tailors interactions to each customer's preferences. For example, ChatGPT can remember if a customer prefers vegan products and suggest relevant items without being asked. This level of personalization makes customers feel valued, enhancing their satisfaction and loyalty. They're not just talking to a robot; they're interacting with a system that knows and cares about their preferences.

Monitor your AI's performance to ensure it performs well. Metrics like response time, resolution rate, and customer satisfaction scores show how well ChatGPT handles interactions. Tools like sentiment analysis can further analyze customer feedback, helping you fine-tune ChatGPT's responses. Regular updates based on these metrics keep your AI system effective and efficient.

Enhancing customer service with AI like ChatGPT isn't just about easing the workload or cutting costs; it's about transforming the customer experience. It provides fast, reliable, and deeply personalized service. AI tools like ChatGPT are invaluable, turning customer service into a dynamic, customer-focused powerhouse. So, as you consider integrating AI into your customer service, view it as an investment in your customers' happiness and your brand's reputation. With AI, every customer interaction becomes an opportunity to impress, engage, and retain.

4.4 Using AI for Project Management: A Game Changer

Project management isn't just about juggling tasks and deadlines; it's like an art form. And, like any good artist, a project manager needs the right tools. Enter AI, the digital equivalent of a Swiss army knife for project managers. Imagine you're planning a major project. The stakes are high, and so is the complexity—AI steps in as a tool and a team member who's always on its game. From setting realistic timelines to ensuring resources are in the right place at the right time, AI has got your back.

Scheduling and Resource Allocation

Let's start with scheduling and resource allocation, which are often headaches for many project managers. AI can look at past project data to predict how long tasks will take and find the best team members for each job based on their skills and previous performance. It's like having a super-smart planner who knows your team's strengths and weaknesses. And it doesn't stop there. AI can keep learning and adjusting these predictions as the project goes on, smoothly adapting to any delays or changes. This means you always have the most accurate forecasts, helping your projects finish on time and stay within budget.

Risk Management

Next is risk management, another critical part of project management where AI shines. Every project has potential problems, but AI can help spot these risks before they become big issues. By looking at data from similar past projects, AI can flag risks that might not be obvious at first. For example, if a certain task missed deadlines in the past, AI can alert you to this pattern so you can plan extra resources or adjust timelines ahead of time. AI can even suggest ways to deal with these risks based on what worked before, tailored to your current project. It's like having a crystal ball that predicts problems and offers solutions.

Enhancing Collaboration

AI can also greatly improve how team members work together. In today's world, where remote work is common, keeping effective communication and collaboration can be tough. AI can help by acting as a central hub for project communication and updates. For instance, AI-driven virtual assistants (like Alexa or Google Assistant) can schedule meetings, send reminders, and provide status updates to team members, keeping everyone on the same page no matter where they are. These assistants can be programmed to understand the project's context and give relevant information to each team member, which boosts efficiency and ensures everyone is focused on what's important.

Real-World Example

Let's look at a real-world example. A tech startup used AI to manage its product development lifecycle. The AI system helped plan sprints, allocate resources, and track progress against deadlines. This helped the startup reduce the time to market by 40% and improved team morale, as team members felt better supported and less stressed about deadlines.

The AI system took care of routine tasks, freeing the team to focus on innovation and problem-solving.

In short, AI in project management isn't just about automating tasks; it's about enhancing the human elements of project management. It lets project managers focus more on strategy and leadership and less on micromanaging tasks and timelines. AI's ability to analyze data, predict trends, and facilitate communication empowers project teams to perform at their best, making project management more efficient and human. AI plays a bigger role in project management, changing how projects are planned, carried out, and completed.

Whether through better planning, risk management, or collaboration, AI is a game-changer in project management. It redefines what teams can achieve when technology and human expertise work together.

4.5 Networking and Building Professional Relationships with AI

Networking might not be your favorite thing. Going to events can feel like being at a high school dance, awkwardly standing around with a drink, hoping someone will talk to you. But what if AI could help? AI-driven networking tools like LinkedIn Sales Navigator can change how we connect, making it less awkward and more meaningful. These tools use smart algorithms to find potential professional contacts that match your career goals and interests. It's like having a matchmaker for your professional life without the awkward first dates.

How AI Networking Tools Work

Imagine you're at a virtual conference. Instead of clicking through random profiles, an AI tool analyzes your professional background and project history to recommend people who share your interests. For example, if you work in renewable energy, the AI might connect you with a solar tech startup founder or an environmental policy analyst. This isn't random; it's about creating opportunities for teamwork and collaboration tailored just for you.

Enhancing Connections with AI

AI doesn't just help you make connections; it also improves them. At virtual conferences, AI can analyze participant lists and find potential matches based on shared interests. It can even schedule meet-ups during the event and automate follow-up communications afterward. It's like having a personal assistant who remembers everyone you met, what you talked about, and when to follow up next.

Maintaining Relationships with AI

Keeping professional relationships going can feel like juggling. AI-powered CRM systems can help you keep track of every interaction, remind you when to check in with contacts, and suggest topics to discuss. For example, if a contact publishes an article, your AI tool will let you know so you can congratulate them and start a conversation about it. This keeps the relationship dynamic and growing without you having to remember everything.

Ethics in AI Networking

Using AI for networking needs to be done responsibly. Ethical AI means being transparent and getting consent. When AI tools suggest connections or gather data, it must be clear and have options for people to opt out. No one likes feeling spied on, so it's important to respect personal boundaries and data privacy.

In the grand scheme of your professional life, AI networking tools are more than just gadgets. They can transform how you connect, interact, and maintain relationships. From finding the right people to talk to, improving online interactions, and keeping track of your network, AI is set to redefine professional networking. So next time you're at a virtual conference or on a networking site, remember: AI could be your best networking buddy, ready to introduce you to people with the ideas, resources, or opportunities you've been looking for.

***

4.6 AI Ethics in the Workplace: What You Need to Know

Introducing AI into the workplace isn't just about boosting efficiency and making tasks easier—it's also about dealing with ethical issues. Think of AI ethics as important as coffee in the break room. It's about ensuring that as AI takes on more roles, it does so transparently, fairly, and responsibly.

Understanding AI Ethics

When we talk about ethical AI, we're talking about the moral guidelines for using AI in the workplace. These guidelines include ensuring transparency, which means explaining how AI systems make decisions. No one likes a mystery box, especially when it can affect someone's job or personal data. It's like a chef who shares their recipe—everyone knows what's going into the dish.

Fairness is also crucial. AI must treat everyone equally and without bias. Imagine a hiring AI that favors candidates from a specific area or school—not cool, right? Ensuring fairness means checking these systems to avoid repeating societal biases.

Accountability ties it all together. A human should always be able to question or override AI decisions. It's like having an emergency stop button on a fast-moving train—it's about safety and making sure there's always a human in control.

Implementing Ethical Practices

To ensure your AI tools follow ethical guidelines, start with clear policies that govern AI use. These rules outline what is and isn't allowed, ensuring everyone plays fair. It's like setting ground rules before a game starts.

Choosing the right AI solutions is also essential. Pick AI tools from developers who prioritize ethical AI development. It's like picking friends who share your values. Also, diverse teams should be involved in developing and using AI systems. This isn't just about inclusivity; diverse teams bring different perspectives, which can help reduce biased AI.

***

Addressing Bias in AI

Bias is a tricky issue. AI systems learn from data, so if that data is biased, the AI's decisions will be too. For example, if a hiring AI is trained on data from a company that mostly hires men, it might favor male candidates. Regularly checking and adjusting AI systems is essential. This means continuously examining the data and decisions to ensure they're as unbiased as possible. Think of it as regular maintenance for your car—it keeps things running smoothly and prevents bigger problems.

Training and Awareness

But here's the thing: this only works if everyone is trained and aware. Everyone from the CEO to the newest intern needs to understand what ethical AI use looks like. This isn't just about workshops or seminars; it's about creating a culture where ethical AI use is as regular as clocking in for the day. It's about making ethics part of the conversation, not an afterthought.

Imagine an office where AI boosts productivity and does so fairly, transparently, and responsibly. Where AI decisions are understood and can be questioned, and bias is continuously reduced. That's the power of ethical AI. It's not just about using AI; it's about using it responsibly.

Get ready for the next chapter, where we'll explore AI's role in specialized fields and how it's changing industries from healthcare to finance. Stay tuned because the AI adventure is just starting, and the best is yet to come!

***

Chapter 4 Exercises:

Exercise 1: AI in Everyday Life

Objective: Identify real-world examples of AI in your daily routine.

Instructions:

1. Think about your daily activities and list five instances where you encounter AI. These could be as simple as using a smartphone app or as complex as interacting with a virtual assistant.

2. For each instance, describe how AI is being used and what benefits it provides.

Exercise 2: Researching AI Tools for Office Automation

Objective: Explore AI tools for automating routine office tasks and compare their features.

Instructions:

1. Research at least three AI tools commonly used for automating office tasks such as data entry, scheduling, or report generation.

2. Create a comparison chart outlining each tool's essential features, compatibility, and user-friendliness.

3. Based on your research, recommend one AI tool you believe would best fit a specific routine task in an office environment and explain your choice.

Exercise 3: Case Study Analysis of AI Integration

Objective: Analyze the impact of AI implementation on office productivity through a real-world case study.

Instructions:

1. Read a case study where AI was used to automate routine tasks in an office setting.

2. Summarize the key findings regarding the impact of AI on productivity and efficiency in the case study.

3. Reflect on how similar AI integration strategies could be applied to enhance productivity in your work environment.

Exercise 4: Task Automation Plan Using AI

Objective: Develop a plan for automating an office's routine tasks using AI.

Instructions:

1. Choose one routine task in an office setting that could be effectively automated using AI.

2. Outline the steps in implementing an AI solution for this task, including tool selection, integration with existing systems, and strategies for monitoring and optimizing the automation process.

3. Present your plan, including the expected benefits and potential challenges of implementing AI for this task.

Exercise 5: Assessing Productivity Impact of AI Automation

Objective: Evaluate the potential impact of AI-driven task automation on office productivity.

Instructions:
1. Create a Mind Map
Step-by-Step Guide:
Set Up Your Mind Map:
- Use a large piece of paper or a digital tool like MindMeister (found in the Google & Apple App stores).

- Write "AI-Driven Task Automation in Offices" in the center.

Identify Key Areas:
- Draw branches for Benefits, Challenges, Real-Life Examples, and Potential Transformations.

Detail the Benefits:
- List advantages like time-saving, error reduction, and allowing employees to focus on creative tasks.

Outline the Challenges:
- Note potential problems like setup costs, job security concerns, and technical issues.

Provide Real-Life Examples:
- Add examples of companies successfully using AI automation, such as chatbots for customer service.

Explore Potential Transformations:
- Think about how AI could change the work environment, such as improving efficiency and employee satisfaction.

Make a Difference with Your Review

Spread the Power of Learning

"The best way to find yourself is to lose yourself in the service of others." - Mahatma Gandhi

Hey there! Have you ever noticed how helping someone else makes you feel really good inside? It's like you're spreading a little bit of sunshine in the world. Well, I've got a tiny favor to ask that can do just that.

Would you help someone who's just getting started with AI, just like you once were?

This person could be anyone—a student, a teacher, a parent, or a curious mind trying to understand what AI is all about. They might be feeling a little lost and need a friendly guide to show them the way.

My goal with this book is to make AI simple and fun for everyone. I want to help as many people as possible see how cool and useful AI can be. But I can't do it alone—I need your help to reach more people.

Here's how you can help: Most people decide if they want to read a book by looking at the reviews. So, I'm asking you to do a quick favor for someone who's just like you—a beginner looking for guidance.

Please take a moment to leave a review for this book.

It won't cost you anything, and it takes less than a minute, but it could mean the world to someone else. Your review might help...

...one more student ace their school project. ...one more parent understand what their kid is talking about. ...one more teacher make their lessons exciting. ...one more curious mind discover a new passion. ...one more dream take flight.

To make a difference and brighten someone's day, all you have to do is... and it only takes 60 seconds... leave a review.

Simply scan the QR code below to leave your review:

[]

If you love the idea of helping someone else, you're in the right place. Welcome to the team. You're one of us now.

I can't wait to keep helping you discover how awesome AI can be. You're going to love the tips and tricks in the rest of this book.

Thanks a bunch! Now, let's get back to the fun stuff.

Chapter Five

Hands-On Projects and Exercises

CHAPTER 5

Imagine you've just been given the keys to a magical toolshed. Inside, you find every tool you need to build something amazing: your very own interactive, AI-powered chatbot. Exciting, right? Get ready because that's what this chapter is all about. Here, I'll guide you through creating your first AI chatbot, one that can chat almost like a real person. Let's get started!

***

5.1 Creating Your First AI Chatbot

Selecting a Platform

Choosing where to build your chatbot is like picking a venue for your birthday party. It must be the right fit, or it won't be fun. There are several platforms, each with different features. When choosing, consider how easy it is to use, especially if you're unfamiliar with coding. Look for platforms with drag-and-drop features; they're super helpful and don't require coding skills.

Next, consider how well the platform works with other tools you use, like your website or social media. You want your chatbot to fit in smoothly, not stick out awkwardly. Also, think about the cost. Many platforms offer free versions with basic features, which are great for beginners.

AI-Powered Chatbot Builders

In today's rapidly evolving digital landscape, building a chatbot has never been more accessible. There are several platforms offering various levels of customization, ease of use, and integration capabilities. Here are some standout options:

ChatGPT and OpenAI

These tools provide powerful language models that can be seamlessly integrated into custom chatbot solutions. Their advanced conversational abilities allow for more natural interactions, making them popular for businesses aiming to enhance customer engagement.

Zapier Chatbots

Zapier lets you quickly create AI chatbots by connecting to your knowledge sources and customizing responses. OpenAI integration and website embedding capabilities offer flexibility for businesses looking to deploy AI-driven solutions without extensive coding.

No-Code/Low-Code Platforms

For those who prefer a faster setup with minimal coding, no-code and low-code platforms provide a viable solution:

1. Chatfuel

- Best For: Facebook Messenger, Instagram, WhatsApp

- Pros: It has a fast and simple setup, a large template library, and a drag-and-drop editor. It also integrates with Zapier, making it easier to connect with various tools.

- Cons: ChatGPT integration could potentially lead to off-topic conversations.

2. MobileMonkey

- Best For: Multi-platform use, including Facebook, Instagram, SMS, and websites

- Features: Offers a unified chat inbox, marketing automation tools, and ready-to-use chatbot templates.

- Pros: Effective for marketing across different business sizes.

- Cons: Could expand integration options further.

3. Botpress

- Best For: Versatile and customizable chatbot development

- Features: Boasts a visual drag-and-drop canvas, automatic translation features, and pre-built integrations for easy deployment.

- Pros: High degree of customization allows businesses to tailor the chatbot's behavior to specific needs.

Designing Conversations

Creating your chatbot's dialogues is like writing a play where your chatbot is the star. You want it to perform well, right? Start by thinking about the types of conversations your chatbot will have. What questions will it need to answer? What responses should it give? This is crucial because a good script leads to great interactions.

Make the conversations feel natural. Nobody likes talking to a robot that sounds like a robot. Use everyday language and a bit of humor if it fits. Also, plan for different paths the conversation could take, like a choose-your-own-adventure book.

Implementing ChatGPT

Now for some tech magic! Integrating ChatGPT into your chatbot makes it come alive. This gives your bot a "brain" that uses its training to generate relevant and human-like responses. Setting up ChatGPT involves accessing OpenAI's API, which might sound complicated, but many platforms make it easy. Test different prompts to see how ChatGPT responds, like rehearsing lines before a play. You want to make sure your chatbot understands and responds well.

Testing and Iterating

The final step is testing and iterating. Just like a play has dress rehearsals, your chatbot needs thorough testing. Start with friends or family and watch how they interact with your bot. Take note of any confusion or glitches. Does the chatbot understand requests? Are the responses engaging? Use this feedback to tweak and improve your chatbot.

Making adjustments based on feedback is like fine-tuning a musical instrument. Each change improves performance. Update the conversational flows, refine the language, and ensure seamless integration with ChatGPT. With each iteration, your chatbot gets more innovative and polished, ready to charm its users.

Creating your first AI chatbot involves selecting the right platform, designing conversations, integrating ChatGPT, and testing and refining. It's about blending technology with creativity to create something that works well and is fun to use. So, let's get building—your first AI chatbot awaits!

5.2 Designing a Simple AI-Driven Survey

Imagine you're a chef trying to figure out why your new mushroom risotto isn't popular. You could guess it's too mushroomy, but guessing won't help. What you need is a good survey, but not just any survey—a smart, AI-driven one that gets you the answers you need. Sounds cool, right? Let's create a survey that's as easy to digest as your mom's spaghetti.

First, define the purpose of your survey. This is your starting point. What do you want to learn? Is it why customers aren't ordering the risotto, or is it general feedback on your menu? Once you have a clear purpose, planning your questions becomes easier. It's like setting your GPS before a trip; it guides every step.

Now, let's craft those questions. This is where AI can help. Using AI tools to generate questions saves you time and ensures they're well-structured. For example, tell the AI your goal is to discover why the mushroom risotto isn't popular. The AI can then generate questions like, "How do you rate the mushroom risotto from 1 to 10?" and "What changes would improve the mushroom risotto for you?" This ensures your questions cover all bases and are easy to understand, giving you useful data.

If you're unsure where to start, here are three survey platforms supporting AI-driven question generation and analysis: [Platform names and details will follow].

And there you have it—a simple, AI-driven survey to get the answers you need!

1. SurveyMonkey Genius:

Features: SurveyMonkey Genius uses AI to help you design, run, and analyze surveys. It has cool features like AI-powered survey creation, predicting the best types of questions to ask, understanding how people feel about their answers, and giving you smart insights to improve your data.

URL: SurveyMonkey Genius

2. SurveySparrow:

Features: SurveySparrow has an AI survey builder that makes creating surveys easier by suggesting questions based on your goals. It includes smart skip logic and AI-powered data analysis through its CogniVue feature, which helps you understand how customers feel and what drives their opinions.

URL: SurveySparrow

3. Responsly:

Features: Responsly lets you create surveys, forms, quizzes, and questionnaires using AI. Its adaptive logic changes the questions based on previous answers for a personalized survey experience. It also offers many integrations and works well on different devices.

URL: Responsly

These platforms use AI to make surveys easier to create, improve the quality of responses, and give you deeper insights through advanced data analysis.

Sample AI-Generated Question List

1. How likely are you to recommend our mushroom risotto to a friend? (Scale of 1-10)

2. What is your favorite dish at our restaurant, and why?

3. Describe your ideal risotto dish.

4. Are there any ingredients you would prefer to be added or removed from our mushroom risotto?

Analyzing Responses with AI

Once your questions are ready, it's time to send them out. But your job isn't done yet. As responses come in, AI helps you analyze the data. This part is like detective work, where AI tools go through the survey answers, finding patterns and insights that might not be immediately obvious. For example, AI might discover that 70% of respondents think the dish needs more seasoning or that it's too filling as a starter. AI analytics can quickly and accurately identify these trends, saving you hours of work and giving you the insights needed to make informed decisions. Think of AI as your assistant, specializing in data instead of desserts.

HANDS-ON PROJECTS AND EXERCISES

Keeping Respondents Engaged

We all know that filling out surveys isn't the most exciting task, so how do you keep it interesting? AI can help personalize the survey for each respondent. For instance, if someone rates the risotto low, the next question could be adjusted to ask more about their reasons rather than asking a generic follow-up question. This dynamic adjustment makes the survey relevant to the respondent, increasing the likelihood of thoughtful, complete answers. It's about making each respondent feel like they're having a conversation, not just filling out a boring form.

With these steps, you're well on your way to creating a survey that's not just a collection of questions but a powerful tool for gathering meaningful data. Whether you're a chef wanting to understand why a dish isn't popular or a business owner seeking customer feedback, an AI-driven survey can provide insights that are valuable and actionable. So, set your goals and let AI take your surveys from boring to insightful. After all, in the world of data, knowledge isn't just power; it's the recipe for success.

5.3 Build a Resume Analyzer Using ChatGPT

Imagine you're a talent scout in a vast forest of job applications, each resume a tree in the dense woods of potential hires. You need a tool to help you find the best candidates quickly. That's where building your resume analyzer with ChatGPT comes in. This tool isn't just a filter; it's like a super-powered magnifying glass that helps you zoom in on the finest details, ensuring you don't miss the hidden gems.

Setting Objectives

First, let's get our goals straight. A resume analyzer is about more than just cutting down the number of resumes you must manually check. It's about spotting the best candidates. This AI-driven tool will sift through piles of resumes to find key skills that match job descriptions, evaluate readability and structure for clarity and professionalism, and match candidates to job descriptions based on compatibility scoring. This last part is like fitting puzzle pieces together; not every piece fits everywhere, but the right ones fit perfectly.

Programming Basics

Now, onto the nuts and bolts—or, in our case, the code and algorithms. Don't worry; you don't need to be a coding expert. ChatGPT can handle most of the heavy lifting with its advanced text analysis capabilities. Your job is to set up a basic framework for ChatGPT to operate. This involves some basic programming, likely in Python, given its simplicity and robust libraries for AI projects.

Start by setting up an environment—like preparing your kitchen before cooking. Then, integrate ChatGPT, essentially inviting this AI helper into your workspace to assist with your task.

Feature Implementation

With the stage set, it's time to add features to this tool. First up, keyword extraction. This is like sending a trained truffle pig into the forest of data; it finds the key terms crucial for the roles you're looking to fill. Next, we implement phrase recognition. This feature helps understand the context of these keywords. It's not enough to know that the word "Python" appears in the resume; you need to see if it refers to programming skills or if the candidate likes watching snake documentaries!

Then, there's compatibility scoring. This is where things get really interesting. The tool scores each candidate on how well they match the job requirements by comparing the extracted keywords and phrases from resumes with the job descriptions. It's like a dating app for jobs and candidates, finding the perfect match based on interests and skills.

Validation and Feedback

Finally, let's ensure this tool is effective. Validation is your reality check. Test the analyzer with real data to see how well it performs. Does it accurately pick up on the required skills? Does it match the right resumes with the correct job descriptions? Feedback from this phase is crucial. It tells you where the gaps are and what needs tweaking. And remember, this tool learns from feedback. You refine its abilities by incorporating input on its performance, much like training a puppy with treats and commands. The more you train it, the better it gets at fetching what you need.

Building a resume analyzer using ChatGPT empowers your recruitment process, making it smarter, faster, and more efficient. By setting clear objectives, laying down a solid programming foundation, implementing robust features, and continually validating and refining the tool, you transform the daunting task of resume review into a streamlined, precision-driven process. This isn't just about saving time; it's about enhancing your ability to discover and attract the best talent. So, get ready to bring the future of recruitment into your hands today. In the competitive world of talent acquisition, having a high-tech tool is not just an advantage; it's a necessity.

5.4 Setting Up an AI-Powered Reminder System

Picture this: You're juggling a million tasks—from feeding the dog to preparing a presentation for next week's big meeting. Wouldn't it be neat to have a smart assistant who reminds you of all these things and knows precisely when to nudge you based on your habits and schedule? Let's design a reminder system smarter than a fifth-grader. This isn't just any reminder system; it's AI-powered, tailored to your life like a custom suit.

System Design

First, the system design—creating a setup that feels like it's reading your mind (in a non-creepy way). The idea is to have AI that doesn't just remind you of set tasks but learns from your behaviors and preferences. For example, if you usually pick up groceries on Saturday mornings, your AI buddy will start to catch on and remind you to grab some eggs and milk before you run out. It's about integrating behavioral analytics, which means the AI understands your patterns and habits. This data helps manage your reminders more effectively, ensuring they're timely and relevant. It's like having a personal assistant who knows your schedule inside out and anticipates your needs.

Integration with Calendars

Integration with calendars is your next stop. If your life is a movie, your calendar is the director—it calls the shots. Integrating your AI reminder system with your existing calendar apps gives your AI system the megaphone to direct your day. Whether you use Google Calendar, Outlook, or another system, the AI will sync with it, ensuring all your appointments, meetings, and personal commitments are in one place. This sync isn't just about convenience; it's about creating a complete view of your time management. When your AI knows you have a meeting until 3 PM but need to pick up your dry cleaning by 5 PM, it can remind you at just the right moment so you're never caught off guard.

User Interaction

Now, how do you talk to this system? It's all about making the interaction as natural as talking to a friend. Most modern AI systems support voice and text commands, so you can set up and manage reminders by speaking or typing a message. You could say, "Hey, remind me to call Mom tomorrow at 7 PM," or type it into your device, and it's done. The system can also ask follow-up questions to clarify details, just like a real assistant would. For instance, if you say, "Set a reminder for the conference," it might ask, "Which conference, and do you need a reminder on the day or the day before?" This back-and-forth ensures your reminders are set up exactly as needed, with no guesswork involved.

Proactive Reminders

Lastly, let's make your reminder system proactive, not just reactive. This means it doesn't just wait for you to tell it what to do; it suggests reminders based on upcoming events or your habits. For example, if you often forget an annual doctor's appointment or a friend's birthday, the AI can track these and give you a heads-up in advance. It learns from past behaviors; if you always call your sister after work on Fridays, it might suggest setting a recurring reminder. This proactive approach means you're always a step ahead, and it feels like your AI truly gets you.

Setting up this AI-powered reminder system is like programming an intelligent, caring robot that ensures you never miss a beat in your busy life. From integrating with your calendars to understanding your habits and even getting proactive with its reminders, this system isn't just about keeping you organized; it's about enhancing your everyday efficiency so you can focus more on enjoying life and less on remembering what comes next. Embrace this digital marvel, and watch as it transforms your chaotic schedule into a well-oiled productivity machine.

5.5 Exercise: Generate a Marketing Campaign with AI

Let's say you've got a brand that's as awesome as a blockbuster summer movie but as unseen as an honest politician. You need not just any marketing campaign but one that's as smart and sleek as a spy gadget you see in those movies. Enter AI, your secret weapon in crafting a marketing campaign that hits the mark and makes a splash. It's time to roll out the red carpet for your brand, and guess what? AI is the director of this show.

First things first, you have to set your campaign objectives. What's the end game here? Are you looking to turn heads and get people talking about your brand? Or is it more about getting likes, shares, and double taps? You may want the town to buzz about your new product launch. Whatever your goal, clearly defining it is your first step. It's like setting the destination before driving; it determines your route and decisions. A well-defined goal is a guiding star, keeping your campaign focused and on track. It ensures every piece of Content, every ad, and every post works hard to achieve your set objectives.

Now, onto the fun part: creating Content. But not just any content; we're talking about Content that pops, sizzles, and sparkles, all thanks to AI's creative genius. Imagine AI as your brainstorming partner who always has ideas. Need a catchy headline? AI's got a dozen. Eye-popping images? AI can help design them. Even videos that tell your brand story can be storyboarded with AI's input. It pulls from a vast database of successful campaigns and current trends to suggest Content that resonates with your audience. It's like having a creative consultant on your team who knows what will click with your audience.

Speaking of the audience, understanding who you're talking to is like knowing whom you're cooking dinner for. You wouldn't serve a steak to a vegetarian, right? AI dives into the ocean of your market data to fish out who your audience is.

It segments them based on demographics, interests, behaviors, and interactions with your brand. This isn't just about knowing their ages and locations but understanding their needs, preferences, and pain points. AI analyses this data to tailor your campaign precisely to match their tastes and expectations. It's about making your audience feel like you get them, creating a campaign that speaks directly to them in a language they understand and appreciate.

Now, you've set sail with your perfectly crafted campaign, but how do you ensure it doesn't veer off course? Here's where AI steps in again, this time as your navigator.

Monitoring a campaign's performance in real-time allows you to see what's working and what's not—like having a GPS that shows your current location and the best routes and shortcuts to your destination. AI tools track various metrics, from engagement rates to click-throughs and conversions. But more than just gathering data, AI interprets it to provide actionable insights. Is one version of an ad performing better than another? AI will spot this and can adjust your campaign automatically, pushing more resources towards what's working best.

This real-time monitoring and adjusting make your marketing campaign responsive and dynamic. It appeals to audience reactions, external factors, and even competitor moves. It's like playing a video game where you can change your strategy on the fly, responding immediately to whatever challenges come your way. This flexibility ensures that your campaign remains effective, no matter how the digital landscape changes, keeping your brand not just in the game but ahead of it.

As you harness AI in your marketing efforts, remember that it's about creating a campaign that reaches and resonates with your audience, turning casual viewers into loyal fans. So, let AI take the wheel, guiding your campaign with precision and creativity, and watch as your brand steps into the spotlight, ready to wow the world.

5.6 Project: Automate Email Responses with ChatGPT

Have you ever felt like a circus performer juggling emails instead of flaming torches? Well, it's time to put down those torches—or at least automate them. Let's dive into creating an automated email response system using ChatGPT that does the heavy lifting for you, ensuring you never drop the ball on communication. This nifty setup isn't just about responding quickly; it's about crafting spot-on replies that your contacts won't even guess it's AI at the keyboard.

Defining Response Rules

First, the ground rules for automation are set. Think of this as laying down the law in the Wild West of your inbox. It would help if you decided when and why ChatGPT should take over. This involves defining trigger keywords or identifying specific senders that might require automated responses. For instance, if you receive an email with the word "appointment," your system can trigger a preset reply confirming receipt and perhaps even links to your calendar.

Similarly, suppose an email comes from a VIP client. In that case, it might automatically trigger a more personalized response, ensuring they're always prioritized. Setting these rules requires some thought. It's about understanding the flow of your usual emails and spotting opportunities where a bit of AI can make life easier.

ChatGPT Integration

Now, let's roll up our digital sleeves and integrate ChatGPT. This step turns your defined rules into action. ChatGPT's prowess in understanding and generating human-like text allows it to craft replies that aren't just generic; they're thoughtful and tailored. Integrating it means setting up ChatGPT with access to your email system through APIs or email processing software. Once done, it's like flipping the switch on a machine that instantly knows how to respond based on the Content of the emails it reads. The key here is to ensure the responses are accurate but also appropriate and helpful. It's like teaching ChatGPT the art of conversation, where it learns the best way to respond in various scenarios, keeping your digital persona professional and courteous.

Here are some valuable resources and guides on integrating ChatGPT into Microsoft Outlook:

- Microsoft Outlook API Documentation

- OpenAI API Documentation

With these resources, you can set up an automated email response system that saves you time and enhances your communication efficiency.

Integration Guides for Automating Email Responses with ChatGPT

1. Zapier Integration Guide
- **Description**: This guide on Zapier explains how to create workflows (called Zaps) to connect Microsoft Outlook with ChatGPT. It walks you through setting up triggers and actions, such as analyzing email content and updating CRM systems.

- **Details**: For more information, visit the Zapier integration guide

2. **The Word 360 Detailed Guide**:
• **Description**: This comprehensive guide covers installing ChatGPT browser extensions, connecting your Outlook account, and using ChatGPT for tasks like drafting emails, scheduling meetings, and setting up automatic responses.
• **Details**: Read the complete guide on The Word 360.

3. **Power Automate Tutorial**:
• **Description**: This tutorial shows how to integrate ChatGPT with Microsoft Outlook using Power Automate. It includes steps for setting up API requests, parsing JSON, and connecting to Outlook for automated workflows.
• **Details**: Watch the tutorial on YouTube.

These resources provide detailed instructions and examples for seamlessly integrating ChatGPT into your Outlook workflow, enhancing productivity, and automating email management.

Handling Complex Queries

Not all emails are easy to answer. Some are like tricky puzzles. To handle these complex queries, you need a plan. First, set complexity rules. If an email has complicated questions or needs a detailed answer, ChatGPT should flag it for you to handle. Think of it like a wrestling match where ChatGPT takes care of the regular moves, but you step in for the special ones. This way, AI handles most emails, and you manage the tough ones, ensuring that everything is clear and personal.

Privacy and Security Considerations

Keeping emails safe is super important. You need to protect the information exchanged when dealing with emails, especially automated responses. Make sure all data handled by ChatGPT follows privacy laws and regulations like GDPR or HIPAA. This means encrypting data, securing access with strong passwords, and regularly checking the system for weaknesses. Think of it as building a strong digital castle to protect your emails from hackers and other threats.

Setting up an automated email response system with ChatGPT is like having a team of virtual assistants who are always ready, never sleep, and handle your emails perfectly. From setting up rules and integrating AI to managing tricky emails and keeping everything secure, this system makes your inbox more efficient and safe.

As we finish this chapter, think about all the projects and exercises we've covered. They are tools to help you use AI in your daily life. Whether you're creating chatbots or automating emails, each project is designed to make things easier and more efficient. Next, we'll explore the ethical side of AI. It's not just about what AI can do but also about using it responsibly and ethically. Stay tuned because this is where it gets really interesting!

Exercise 1: Creating Your First AI Chatbot

Objective: Build and implement an AI chatbot using a user-friendly platform, integrating ChatGPT for enhanced interactions.

Instructions:

Step 1: Choosing a Platform
- Look for platforms that let you create a chatbot by dragging and dropping elements.
- Compare a few options and pick the one that suits your needs best.

Step 2: Designing Your Chatbot Conversations
- Create a flowchart showing how your chatbot will talk to users, including different paths users can take.
- Write example conversations for these paths in a friendly and natural way.

Step 3: Adding ChatGPT to Your Chatbot
- Learn how to include ChatGPT in your chosen platform.
- Test the chatbot by typing different messages and see how it responds.
- Make adjustments to make the chatbot's answers sound more human-like.

Step 4: Testing and Improving
- Ask three people to interact with your chatbot and gather their feedback.
- Make changes to your chatbot's conversations and ChatGPT integration based on the feedback you receive.

Exercise 2: Designing a Simple AI-Driven Survey

Objective: Create an AI-driven survey to gather valuable feedback and analyze the data using AI tools.

Instructions:

1. Defining the Purpose:
• Clearly state the purpose of your survey and what you aim to learn from it.
• List three specific objectives you want to achieve with the survey results.

2. Crafting Questions:
• Use an AI tool to generate at least five survey questions relevant to your objectives.
• Review and refine the questions to ensure they are clear and relevant.

3. **Deploying the Survey:**
• Choose a survey platform that supports AI-driven question generation and analysis.
• Set up the survey and distribute it to your target audience.
• Monitor the response rate and engagement.

4. **Analyzing Responses:**
• Use AI tools to analyze the survey responses, identifying patterns and insights.

Exercise 3: Build a Resume Analyzer Using ChatGPT

Objective: Develop an AI tool to analyze resumes and match candidates to job descriptions efficiently.

Instructions:

1. **Setting Objectives:**

• Outline what you want your resume tool to achieve, such as spotting important details and checking compatibility.
• List the key features you need to make these goals a reality.

2. Getting Started:
• Lay down the basics for your project in simple terms without diving into technical details.
• Make sure you have a good plan for how your tool will work.

3. Essential Features:
• Focus on adding functions like finding keywords and understanding relevant information from resumes.
• Create a way to compare resumes with job descriptions accurately.
• Test these functions with different sample resumes and job requirements to see how well they work.

4. Testing and Improvements:
• See how well your tool works by trying it out with real resumes.

- Ask for feedback on how accurate and helpful the tool is.
- Use the feedback to make your tool better and more effective.

Exercise 4: Setting Up an AI-powered Reminder System

Objective: Create an easy-to-use reminder system using AI to help you remember tasks and schedules better.

Steps to Follow:

1. **Planning the System**
   - **List Important Features:**

- Make a list of what your reminder system should do. For example:
- Remind you of appointments
- Suggest when to do tasks
- Alert you about upcoming deadlines

Explain How the System Learns:

- Think about how the system can learn from your habits. For example:
- If you usually exercise in the evening, the system can remind you to exercise around that time.

It will notice if you often reschedule meetings and adjust reminders accordingly.

2. **Connecting with Calendars**
   - **Pick a Calendar:**

- Choose a calendar app you already use, like Google Calendar or Outlook.

   - **Link Your AI System:**

- Use a simple tool or app to connect your calendar to the reminder system. Many tools offer easy integration without needing to write any code. Some examples include:
- IFTTT (If This Then That)
- Zapier

   - **Ensure Access:**

- Make sure your reminder system can see your calendar events and add new reminders. This usually involves permitting the calendar settings.

3. **Talking to Users**
   - **Design User Interaction:**

- Create a simple interface for setting and managing reminders. This could be through:
- A mobile app
- A web app
- A voice assistant like Google Assistant or Amazon Alexa
  - **Add Command Options**:

- Allow users to give commands by voice or text. For instance:
- "Remind me to buy groceries tomorrow at 6 PM."
- "What's on my schedule for today?"

Test User Interaction:

- Try out the commands yourself to make sure they work smoothly. Ask friends or family to test them, too, and give feedback.

4. *Coming Up with Reminders*
- **Teach the System:**

- Set up the AI to suggest reminders based on your habits. For example:
- If you have a recurring meeting every Monday, the system can remind you to prepare for it on Sunday.
  - **Test and Improve**:

- Pretend to be a user and see if the reminders make sense. For example:
- If you always need a reminder to take out the trash on Thursday, check if the system suggests

Exercise 5: Generate a Marketing Campaign with AI

Objective: Create a simple, AI-driven marketing campaign to promote a brand or product.

Instructions:

1. Setting Campaign Objectives
- **Define the Primary Goals:**

- **Task**: Think about what you want to achieve with your marketing campaign.
- **Example**: Do you want more people to know about your brand, or are you launching a new product?
  - **List Specific, Measurable Objectives:**

HANDS-ON PROJECTS AND EXERCISES

- **Task**: Write down clear goals that you can measure.
- **Example**: Increase website visits by 20% in three months or get 500 new followers on social media.

2. Creating Content

- **Use AI Tools for Ideas:**

- **Task**: Use simple AI tools to help you develop content ideas, catchy headlines, and attractive images.
- **Example** Tools: Canva for visual content, Copy.ai for headlines and text ideas.

- **Develop a Content Calendar:**

- **Task**: Plan when and where you will post your Content.
- **Example**: Create social media posts, blog articles, and email newsletters..

- **Ensure Content Matches Goals:**

- **Task**: Ensure everything you create helps you reach your campaign goals.
  - **Example**: If your goal is brand awareness, create Content that tells your brand's story and shares what makes it unique.

3. Understanding the Audience

- **Analyze Your Audience:**

- **Task**: Use simple AI tools to learn more about the people you want to reach.
- **Example Tools**: Facebook Insights or Google Analytics to see who visits your site or likes your posts.

- **Segment the Audience:**

- **Task**: Group your audience into segments based on their interests and behaviors.
- **Example**: Create one group for young adults interested in tech and another for parents looking for educational products.

- **Tailor Content for Each Segment:**

- **Task:** Make different content for each group to match their preferences.

Example: Share tech news, gadgets for young adults, and educational tips and products for parents.

4. Monitoring and Adjusting

- **Set Up AI Tools for Monitoring:**

- **Task**: Use AI tools to monitor how your campaign is doing in real-time.
- **Example Tools**: Hootsuite for social media, Google Analytics for website traffic.
  - **Track Key Metrics:**

- **Task**: Keep track of important numbers like how many people see your Content, click on your links, or buy your product.
- **Example Metrics**: Engagement rates, click-through rates, and sales conversions.
  - **Adjust Based on Data:**

- **Task**: Change your campaign as needed based on what the data shows.
- **Example**: If a specific post type is prevalent, create more content like that.

By following these steps, beginners can create an effective, AI-driven marketing campaign that efficiently promotes their brand or product.

Exercise 6: Automate Email Responses with ChatGPT

Objective: Set up an easy-to-use automated email response system using ChatGPT to improve communication efficiency.

Instructions:

1. **Defining Response Rules**
   - **Identify Common Email Scenarios:**

- **Task**: Think about the types of emails you usually receive. These could be appointment requests, customer inquiries, or order confirmations.
- **Example**: For customer inquiries, you might receive emails asking about product details or shipping information.
  - **List Trigger Keywords and Specific Senders:**

- **Task**: Write down keywords that can trigger an automated response. Also, list any essential senders that always need a quick reply.
- **Example**: Trigger keywords could be "appointment," "order status," or "support."

2. **ChatGPT Integration**
   - **Follow a Guide to Integrate ChatGPT:**

- **Task**: Use an online tutorial to help you connect ChatGPT with your email system. Tools like Zapier or Integromat can simplify this process without needing to code.

HANDS-ON PROJECTS AND EXERCISES

- **Example Resource**: Zapier Guide to Email Automation
  - **Test the Integration**:

- **Task**: Send some test emails to see how ChatGPT responds. Check if the responses make sense and are helpful.
- **Example**: Email the subject "appointment" and see if ChatGPT sends a confirmation reply.
  - **Adjust Settings:**

- **Task**: If the responses aren't perfect, tweak the settings. This might mean changing the trigger words or adjusting the response content.
- **Example**: If the reply to an "appointment" email is too formal, you can edit it to be more casual.

3. Handling Complex Queries
   - **Define Parameters for Complex Queries:**

- **Task**: Decide which types of emails need a human touch and can't be handled by ChatGPT alone.
- **Example**: Emails with detailed questions or unusual requests should be flagged for manual review.
  - **Flag and Escalate These Queries:**

- **Task**: Set up a system that marks these complex emails for you to handle personally.
- **Example**: Use your email system's filtering feature to send flagged emails to a separate folder.

4. Privacy and Security Considerations
   - **Ensure Compliance with Privacy Laws:**

- **Task**: Ensure your email automation complies with privacy laws like the General Data Protection Regulation (GDPR) or California Consumer Privacy Act (CCPA).
- **Example Resource**: GDPR Compliance Guide
  - **Implement Data Encryption and Secure Access:**

- **Task**: Use tools that encrypt your emails and ensure only authorized people can access them.
- **Example**: Enable encryption settings in your email service and use strong passwords.
  - **Regularly Audit the System:**

- **Task**: Check your system regularly to ensure it's secure and working well.
- **Example**: Set a reminder to review your email automation settings every month.

Following these beginner-friendly steps, you can set up an automated email response system that saves time and improves communication efficiency with ChatGPT.

Chapter Six

Addressing Ethical Considerations

CHAPTER 6

Imagine you've just bought a cool new gadget that promises to make your life super easy. Exciting, right? Now, imagine if that gadget started making decisions for you without asking. That might feel a little weird, right? This is what happens with AI if we don't think about ethics, especially AI bias. It's like having a smart assistant who decides to play loud music at 3 AM because you liked a similar song once. Not fun, right?

6.1 Understanding AI Bias and How to Mitigate It

What Is AI Bias

AI bias happens when an AI system makes unfair decisions because of faulty programming. Imagine your music app only suggesting songs from the same two artists because they were the first you listened to. These biases can sneak in through the data the AI learns from, the way it's programmed, and the goals it's given. Just like listening to the same songs over and over can be annoying, AI bias can lead to unfair outcomes.

Sources of AI Bias

AI bias usually starts with the data it learns from. If the data is biased, the AI will be too. For example, if a facial recognition system is only trained on pictures of one race or age group, it won't work well for others. Similarly, if an AI that screens job applications learns from biased hiring data, it will continue those biases.

How to Fix AI Bias

To fix AI bias, we need several strategies. First, use diverse training data, like adding more spices to a recipe to make it better. Second, use bias detection algorithms to find and fix biased decisions. Finally, having diverse teams work on AI projects can help spot biases that others might miss.

Real-World Example

A famous AI recruiting tool favored male candidates over female ones because it learned from resumes mostly submitted by men. To fix this, the company added more diverse resume examples and regularly checked the AI's decisions for fairness. This made the hiring process fairer and improved the company's reputation.

Navigating the ethics of AI is like solving a complex puzzle. It takes effort, creativity, and a commitment to fairness. By understanding and fixing AI bias, we can ensure our AI systems treat everyone fairly, making the future of technology exciting and just.

6.2 Privacy Concerns with AI: What You Should Know

Ever thought about how much personal info you share with apps and websites? From birthday party photos to late-night food cravings, your digital footprint is everywhere. Now, add AI to the mix, and things get even more interesting. AI loves data, but the line between cool and creepy can blur as AI gets smarter.

AI systems process lots of personal data to learn and make predictions. This can be cool, like your phone, knowing you're about to text your friend. However, if this data is mishandled, it could lead to privacy issues like unauthorized tracking or identity theft. That's why understanding AI and data privacy is so important.

Privacy Rules

Laws like GDPR and CCPA protect your data. GDPR gives EU citizens control over their data, allowing them to ask companies what data they have and to delete it if needed. CCPA provides similar protections for Californians. These laws ensure companies handle your data responsibly.

Protecting Your Data

To protect your data, use anonymization, which hides your identity. Secure data storage keeps your data safe, and privacy by design means building products with privacy in mind from the start. This way, your data stays protected.

Emerging AI Trends

As AI evolves, new privacy concerns arise. Facial recognition is cool for unlocking phones but can be creepy if used without consent. AI in healthcare can improve treatments, but sensitive health data must be handled carefully. Keeping privacy at the forefront ensures these advancements don't compromise your privacy.

Understanding how AI interacts with your data can help you enjoy digital perks without worrying about privacy. Keep using your AI assistants, but be mindful of sharing too much personal info.

6.3 The Future of AI: Ethical Considerations and Predictions

Looking into the future of AI is exciting and mysterious. We imagine AI systems managing our homes, making scientific breakthroughs, and much more. But as these technologies advance, they bring up ethical questions that could impact society.

Imagine an AI that books your doctor's appointments and predicts health risks. This could revolutionize medicine but raises concerns about autonomy. How much control should AI have over personal decisions? These are important questions as AI becomes more integrated into our lives.

Preparing for Ethical Challenges

Education is key to understanding and addressing these ethical challenges. Engaging experts from different fields helps provide a comprehensive view of AI's impact. This ensures we build AI systems that are both technically proficient and ethically sound.

Governance

Just like cities have traffic rules, we need clear guidelines for developing and using AI responsibly. These frameworks create an environment where ethical AI development can thrive. They should set standards, provide data usage guidelines, and ensure AI systems are accountable. Governance frameworks must evolve with technology to address new ethical issues.

Navigating the future of AI is like exploring uncharted waters. The potential for innovation is huge, but so are the risks. By preparing for ethical challenges and establishing strong governance, we can steer AI towards a future that reflects our values. As we embrace this AI-driven horizon, let's do so with wisdom, foresight, and responsibility, ensuring AI's future benefits everyone.

6.4 Transparency in AI: Why It Matters

Imagine the last time you followed a GPS to a new restaurant, only to end up at a dead-end street. Frustrating, right? What if your GPS could explain exactly why it made that mistake—like saying it hadn't updated its maps in a while? That little bit of honesty wouldn't get you to dinner faster, but it would help you understand what went wrong. The same goes for AI systems. Understanding why AI makes certain decisions is crucial when those decisions impact our lives, like with job applications or loan approvals. It's not just about making AI less mysterious; it's about trust, accountability, and making sure these systems aren't leading us down a digital dead-end.

Achieving transparency in AI isn't just nice; it's a must, especially in areas where decisions have significant consequences. But how do we make these complex systems more understandable? One way is through open-source algorithms. Think of it like a community garden; by allowing everyone to see and contribute to the coding (like planting, weeding, and harvesting), the whole community benefits from shared knowledge and oversight. This transparency builds trust and improves the algorithms, as diverse perspectives help identify and correct issues more efficiently than any single coder could.

Another method is explainable AI (XAI). This is where AI tries to break down its process into terms humans can understand. It's like a magician revealing the secrets behind a trick. Instead of sawed-in-half people, we get insights into how AI processes data and arrives at conclusions. Explainable AI helps make the decision-making processes of AI systems more accessible and understandable to the users they serve.

Comprehensive documentation of AI systems also plays a crucial role. This involves keeping detailed records of the system's development, training, and deployment. Think of it as the instruction manual that comes with your high-tech toaster, detailing everything from how it toasts your bread to troubleshooting when all it gives you is charred crumbs.

However, understanding AI's thought process has its challenges. One major hurdle is the complexity of these systems. AI, especially deep learning models, can be as intricate as a jigsaw puzzle with a million pieces. Making this understandable to non-experts is a considerable feat. Then there's the issue of proprietary technologies. Many companies see their AI algorithms as secret recipes, which they guard fiercely to maintain competitive edges. This secrecy can directly oppose the push for openness and transparency.

So, how do we navigate these challenges? Education and regulation play significant parts. By educating AI creators and users about the importance of transparency, we cultivate a community that values and demands clear explanations. Much like rules in sports, regulation sets the boundaries within which AI must operate transparently. It ensures that companies can't just claim their AI is too complex to explain or too proprietary to expose.

There are great examples of increased transparency leading to better outcomes. AI systems that explain how they diagnose or recommend treatments have seen higher acceptance among doctors and patients, leading to better healthcare delivery. On the other hand, systems that fail to justify their decisions have sometimes led to misdiagnoses and a reluctance among healthcare professionals to use AI tools, underscoring the importance of transparency.

Making AI transparent ensures it acts responsibly in our digital society. It's about maintaining human oversight in a world increasingly run by algorithms. By striving for clear, understandable, and open AI systems, we ensure that these powerful tools are not just serving the few who understand them but are accountable and understandable to all of us. As we continue integrating AI into every corner of our lives, let's commit to keeping these systems as transparent as the intentions behind their creation. This commitment enhances our control over these digital forces and ensures they contribute positively to society, paving the way for a future where technology and transparency walk hand in hand.

6.5 Misuse of AI: A Critical Issue

Let's talk about something serious about AI: misuse. Imagine using a famous Picasso painting as a doormat. That sounds pretty ridiculous, right? Now, think about someone misusing powerful AI technology in the same way. AI has the potential to change our lives for the better, but in the wrong hands, it can create really bad situations, like something out of a scary movie. From fake videos that can ruin someone's reputation to surveillance systems that spy on people, the misuse of AI can have serious consequences.

***

Deepfakes and Surveillance

One of the most well-known misuses of AI is deepfakes. These are videos or audio recordings that use AI to make it look or sound like someone is saying or doing something they never did. It's like a super-powered ventriloquism act. Another misuse of AI is in surveillance. Without proper rules, AI can turn security cameras into tools that invade privacy, watching people's every move without their permission. And let's not forget information manipulation, where AI algorithms can be changed to show you only certain types of news or ads, subtly shaping your opinions and decisions.

Preventing Misuse

Stopping the misuse of AI isn't as simple as just putting digital handcuffs on it. It requires smart technology solutions and strict rules, along with everyone agreeing to follow ethical guidelines. Technologically, we can use things like watermarking digital content to show when AI has been used to alter it. This is like putting a label on food packaging to tell you it's been genetically modified. On the regulatory side, laws must be as flexible and up-to-date as the technology they control, closing any loopholes that could lead to misuse.

Ethical Guidelines

Ethical guidelines act as a moral compass for AI development and use. They help keep AI developers and users from crossing into ethically questionable areas. But these guidelines shouldn't just be words on a poster. They need to be part of every stage of AI systems, from design to deployment. Education and awareness are also crucial. Just like you need to learn the rules of the road before driving, understanding the ethical implications of AI is essential before using its power. This means teaching ethical AI use to tech developers, students, and company leaders.

A Team Effort

Stopping AI misuse requires teamwork between governments, industries, and the public. Think of it as a neighborhood watch program but for AI. Governments can set the rules, industries can follow best practices, and the public can stay informed and report abuses. Together, this collaborative effort can ensure AI is used responsibly, maximizing benefits while minimizing harms. This is not just about avoiding the dark future shown in movies; it's about building a future where AI is a positive force, benefiting society while respecting our values and rights.

6.6 Ethical AI Usage: Best Practices for Beginners

Stepping into the world of AI can feel like being the new kid in a futuristic neighborhood. It's exciting, a bit scary, and full of possibilities. As you explore this new world, it's important to have a moral compass—ethics. Think of ethical AI like seasoning in cooking; without it, things can turn bland or even bad. So, let's add some ethical seasoning to your AI work, making sure you use this powerful technology fairly, responsibly, and with respect for human rights.

Fairness

Fairness in AI means ensuring that AI systems treat all users equally. It's like making sure everyone at the dinner table gets an equal slice of pie—no one wants to get the smallest piece. Fairness ensures everyone has the same opportunities and outcomes from AI systems.

Accountability

Accountability means being able to trace decisions made by AI back to someone who can take responsibility. It's like knowing who to call if your pizza delivery goes wrong. Someone needs to be responsible for the AI's actions.

Respect for Human Rights

Respect for human rights in AI usage ensures that these technologies support and enhance human dignity, freedom, and cultural diversity rather than undermining them. It's about using AI to help people, not harm them.

How to Implement Ethical AI

Choose the Right Tools: Just like you wouldn't use a sledgehammer to crack a nut, select AI technologies known for their ethical integrity. Choose transparent AI systems that are open about how they operate and use data. Look for AI tools that have undergone bias and fairness audits.

Set Clear Guidelines: Ensure that the AI's decisions are fair and just by setting clear guidelines on what the AI should and shouldn't do. For example, if you're using AI for hiring, set rules to prevent it from making decisions based on sensitive attributes like age, gender, or race. It's like setting ground rules at a party—everyone knows what's cool and what's not, making for a better experience.

Monitor and Evaluate: Keep an eye on your AI, like watching a pot on the stove. Regularly check that the AI behaves as expected and doesn't stray into unethical territory. Use tools like audits and impact assessments to understand how your AI affects different groups of people. This ongoing caution helps catch any ethical slips before they turn into bigger problems.

By following these best practices, you can navigate the exciting world of AI responsibly, ensuring your work is fair, accountable, and respectful of human rights.

Ethical AI Resources and Best Practices

If you want to learn more about using AI ethically, there are tons of resources to help you out. Online courses from places like Coursera Coursera and edX cover the basics of ethical AI. You can also join community groups on platforms like Meetup or LinkedIn to connect with other people who care about AI ethics. These resources offer a wealth of information and support, helping you stay informed and connected as AI technology evolves.

As you use AI in your life or work, remember that using AI ethically is not just a good practice—it's essential. It ensures that the technology improves lives and operates fairly, responsibly, and respectfully. By following ethical guidelines, you protect your projects from moral issues and contribute to a culture of ethical technology use, inspiring others to do the same.

Navigating the ethical aspects of AI is like learning to drive. You start slow, learn the rules, and gradually build your confidence. You might make a few mistakes along the way, but with the right approach and resources, you'll be on your way, knowing you're handling your AI projects with care and integrity. As you move forward, keep these ethical practices in mind—they are your roadmap to a successful and responsible AI journey.

***

Exercises for Chapter 6: Addressing Ethical Considerations

Understanding AI Bias

Objective: Learn about AI bias and understand its sources and mitigation strategies.

Exercise 1: Defining AI Bias

1. **Task**: Define AI bias in your own words.

• **Example Answer**: "AI bias is when an AI system makes unfair decisions because it has learned from biased data or has been programmed in a way that favors certain groups over others."

1. **Task:** Provide an example of AI bias.

• **Example Answer**: "An example of AI bias is a hiring algorithm that favors male candidates over female candidates because it was trained on resumes predominantly submitted by men.

Exercise 2: Sources and Mitigation of AI Bias

1. **Task:** List three sources of AI bias and explain how each can influence AI decision-making.

- **Example Answers**:

• **Biased Training Data:** If the data used to train the AI is not diverse and representative, the AI will learn these biases and make decisions that reflect them.

- **Flawed Programming:** If the algorithms are written with certain assumptions, they can unintentionally favor specific outcomes.
- **Unintended Bias from Objective Setting:** If the AI's goals are biased, it will work towards these biased outcomes, perpetuating unfair practices.

2. **Task:** Explain the concept of diversifying training data using an analogy.
    - **Example Analogy:** Diversifying training data is like adding various spices to a recipe. Just as different spices enhance the flavor and balance of a dish, diverse data ensures that AI makes fair and balanced decisions.

Chapter Seven

Keeping Up with AI Developments

CHAPTER 7

Imagine you're a treasure hunter, not the old-school type who wades through dark caves with a torch, but a modern-day digital explorer, seeking out the most precious gems of information in the sprawling, ever-changing landscape of Artificial Intelligence. Keeping up with AI is more than staying current; it's about staying ahead and caught up when the next big AI wave comes crashing in. So, how do you keep your finger on the pulse of AI innovations without getting overwhelmed? Let's dive in—or rather, let's calmly wade into the waters of AI developments together.

***

7.1 Following AI Innovations: Best Sources and Practices

Find the Best AI News Websites

First, let's talk about where to find the best AI news. Not all websites are equal, so it's important to know the top ones. TechCrunch, Wired, and The Verge are great places to start. They report on the latest AI developments and explain why they matter to you.

For deeper insights, check out MIT Technology Review and Ars Technica. These sites dive into how AI is changing industries like healthcare and finance. They have case studies, interviews, and expert opinions that give you a full view of the AI world.

Use Social Media Wisely

Next, let's talk about social media. Twitter and LinkedIn are your go-to platforms here. You can follow AI experts like Andrew Ng or Fei-Fei Li for the latest updates and insights. It's like having a direct line to the people shaping AI.

Don't just scroll through your feed—engage! Reply to posts, ask questions, and share articles. The AI community is very interactive, and you can learn a lot by participating.

Set Up Alerts and Feeds

To ensure you never miss anything important, set up Google Alerts for AI topics. It's like having a personal assistant finding AI news for you. Use keywords like "AI advancements," "machine learning updates," or "neural network innovations."

Here's how to set up Google Alerts:

1. Go to the Google Alerts website.

2. Enter your search query or keywords related to AI topics.

3. Customize the alert settings, like frequency, sources, language, and region.

4. Enter your email address.

5. Click the "Create Alert" button.

You can also use RSS feeds to subscribe to AI blogs and websites. This way, all the news comes to one place, like your personalized news ticker.

Check Information Credibility

In the digital age, not everything you read is true. To find reliable information, consider the source. Reputable publications and authors with a good track record in tech journalism are usually trustworthy. Look for citations and references that back up their claims.

Remember, the world of AI changes quickly. Today's big news can be old news tomorrow. So, keep your information up-to-date and accurate.

AI Trend Tracker

To keep up with AI trends, I've included a simple tool to help you track them. This will bring the latest AI trends to your digital doorstep. Follow these steps to stay informed and ahead in the world of AI.

Beginner'sGuide to Tracking AI Trends

Objective: Learn how to track AI trends using beginner-friendly tools and resources.
   Steps to Track AI Trends
   1. **Set Up News Alerts**
      - **Google Alerts**:

      - **Task**: Use Google Alerts to get email notifications about new articles on AI topics

   - **Steps**:
   1. Go to Google Alerts.

2. Enter AI-related keywords like "artificial intelligence," "machine learning," or "deep learning."

3. Set how often you want alerts and where they come from.

4. You'll get emails when new articles are published.

2. **Use Online Platforms**
   - Feedly:

   - **Task**: Collect news from different sources in one place.

   - **Steps**:

   1. Sign up for a free account on Feedly.

   2. Follow AI topics and publications.

   3. Customize your feed to show the latest AI articles and updates.

   - **Reddit**:

• **Task**: Follow AI-related subreddits to stay updated on discussions and news.

• **Steps**:

   1. Go to Reddit.

   2. Subscribe to subreddits like r/artificial, /MachineLearning, and r/deeplearning.

   3. Join discussions and follow the latest trends and news.

3. **Explore AI News Websites**
   - **Task**: Visit websites focused on AI news and updates.

   - **Examples**:

   1. AI News: Offers many articles on AI advancements.

   2. MIT Technology Review: Provides in-depth articles on AI research and trends.

   3. Towards Data Science: Features articles and tutorials on AI and machine learning.

4. **Social Media**

- **X (aka Twitter):**

  - **Task**: Follow AI experts and organizations on Twitter.

  - **Steps**: Find and follow people and groups that post about AI.

5. **Join AI Communities**
   - **Task**: Join online communities where AI topics are discussed.

   - **Examples**:

     1. Kaggle: A community for data scientists and AI enthusiasts.

     2. AI Alignment Forum: Discusses the future and safety of AI.

Summary

Using these beginner-friendly tools and resources allows you to effectively track AI trends and stay informed about the latest developments. Set up Google Alerts, use Feedly and Reddit, explore AI news websites, follow AI experts on Twitter, and join AI communities to engage with the AI world. This approach will help you navigate the vast ocean of AI information and stay updated on current trends and innovations.

7.2 Participating in AI and ChatGPT Online Communities

Dive into the lively world of AI and ChatGPT online communities! These are places where fans, experts, and newcomers come together on forums, social media, and special networking sites. Think of these communities as busy digital cafés, where every table is full of conversations about the latest breakthroughs, challenges, and the future of AI. Websites like Stack Overflow and GitHub and subreddits like r/MachineLearning and r/Artificial are hotspots buzzing with fresh ideas and innovations. You can almost hear the clatter of keyboards as people from all over the world share insights, ask tough questions, and provide helpful answers, building a huge pool of collective knowledge.

Why Join AI and ChatGPT Communities?

Learning from Others: These communities are like 24/7 study groups. You can learn from real-world experiences and case studies shared by others. Have a question at 2 AM? Please post it in a forum; you might have several answers by breakfast.

Getting Support: AI can be complicated, like solving a Rubik's cube blindfolded. These communities offer support, helping you understand complex topics and guiding you when you get stuck.

Collaboration Opportunities: Many members seek collaboration on projects, from academic research to startup ventures. Engaging in these communities can open doors to new opportunities, like working on a project with a coder from Sweden and a data scientist from Singapore, potentially revolutionizing how small businesses use chatbots.

Contributing: Don't just read; share your own experiences, no matter how small they seem. Your information could be the missing piece someone else needs. Ask insightful questions, offer answers, and share articles or code snippets. Your voice matters, and your unique perspective could help others.

Community Etiquette

Each platform has guidelines, but some core values remain essential: respect, openness to diverse opinions, and professional behavior. Think of it as attending a global conference. Present your ideas respectfully and constructively. Constructive criticism can help others grow, but harsh comments can stop discussions and innovation.

Becoming an Active Member

Participating in AI and ChatGPT communities turns you from a solitary learner into a connected, contributing member of a dynamic network. You're not just keeping up with AI; you're shaping its conversation, building your reputation, and expanding your knowledge. So, sign up, log in, and start engaging. The digital world of AI and ChatGPT is waiting for your contributions. Who knows? Your next post could be the start of something groundbreaking.

7.3 Continuous Learning in AI: Online Courses and Resources

Starting to learn more about AI through online courses is like entering a theme park with many paths to explore, each offering its own excitement. But just like you wouldn't go on every ride without a plan (especially the intense ones after a big meal), choosing the right AI courses requires strategy. It's not just about picking the most popular one. Find a course that matches your skills, learning goals, and schedule.

First, let's talk about picking the right courses. You need to know where you are in your AI learning journey. Are you just starting, or do you have some experience with AI projects? This self-check helps you find courses that match your level. Beginners should look for classes covering the basics, like AI terminology and simple programming. You can explore topics like machine learning algorithms or deep learning if you're more advanced. Platforms like Coursera, edX, and Udacity offer courses from top universities and companies, like having a trusted guide for your learning adventure.

Next, let's discuss free vs. paid resources. Free courses are great for getting a feel for AI without spending money. They let you explore different areas of AI without the pressure of paying. But they might not be as detailed or offer the personal help you need to advance. Paid courses often give you more structured learning, hands-on projects, and sometimes even a mentor. It's like investing in a high-quality map before you go hiking—it helps you navigate better.

Building your AI knowledge is like climbing a ladder. You start with the basics and slowly move up to more complex topics. Structured learning paths are helpful because they build your skills step-by-step. Begin with foundational courses to get a strong understanding of AI. Once you're comfortable, move to intermediate topics that challenge you, then advance to specialized subjects. This way, you build a solid and scalable knowledge base in AI.

And don't forget about certifications. Completing a course is great, but having a certificate to show for it is even better. It's like a golden ticket. It proves your dedication and skills, which can be valuable to employers or collaborators. Certifications from recognized platforms can boost your professional credibility and show that you're serious about AI. These credentials can be very persuasive for those wanting to switch careers or advance in tech roles.

7.4 Conferences and Workshops on AI You Should Not Miss

If you're serious about AI, attending AI conferences is essential. These events are where AI experts share their knowledge, and enthusiasts like us gather to learn and network. From the bright lights of Las Vegas to the historic streets of London, these conferences are full of innovation and collaboration. Key events like Neural Information Processing Systems (NeurIPS), the International Conference on Machine Learning (ICML), and the AI World Conference offer more than just the latest breakthroughs; they provide a chance to engage with the people shaping the future of AI.

Preparing for these conferences is like getting ready for a marathon. It's important to be well-prepared. Start by identifying the sessions that match your interests or areas where you need more knowledge. Most conferences publish their schedules in advance so you can plan. Make a list of must-attend workshops and keynotes. These events are often where groundbreaking research is presented or significant announcements are made. Also, try to attend some sessions outside your usual interests—you might discover new passions or gain unexpected insights.

Networking is the key to making the most of any conference. Prepare questions you want to ask about the latest trends in machine learning, ethical AI, or AI applications in healthcare or finance. Having these questions ready can help you start conversations. The goal is to build connections that could lead to collaborations, job opportunities, or finding a mentor. Bring plenty of business cards, and consider using a digital business card that can be shared via smartphones.

Exercise: Networking at an AI Conference

Objective: Prepare for effective networking at an AI conference by preparing key questions and ensuring you can share your contact information.

    Instructions:
    1. Prepare Key Questions
    Step-by-Step Guide:
        1. **Identify Topics of Interest:**

- **Task:** Think about what you're most curious about regarding AI.

- **Examples:**

  - Latest trends in machine learning

  - Ethical considerations in AI

  - AI applications in healthcare or finance

1. **Craft Your Questions:**

- **Task:** Write down at least three questions for each topic you're interested in.

- **Example Questions:**

  - What are the new trends in machine learning this year?

  - How are companies handling ethical issues in AI development?

  - Can you share any recent breakthroughs in AI for healthcare?

1. **Review and Refine:**

- **Task:** Make sure your questions are clear and open-ended to encourage conversation.

- **Tip:** Avoid yes/no questions to promote deeper discussions.

2. Prepare to Share Your Contact Information

Step-by-Step Guide:

1. **Create Business Cards:**

- **Task:** Ensure you have plenty of business cards with your contact information.

- **Tip:** Include your name, title, email, phone number, and LinkedIn profile.

1. **Consider Digital Business Cards:**

- **Task:** Set up a digital business card that can be easily shared via smartphones.

- **Example Tools:**

  - HiHello: Digital Business Cards

- **QR Code Generator:** Create a QR code that links to your contact information.

1. **Practice Your Introduction:**

- **Task:** Prepare a brief introduction about yourself, your interests, and your goals.

- **Example:** "Hi, I'm [Your Name], a [Your Position] with a keen interest in AI applications in healthcare. I'm particularly curious about recent innovations and ethical considerations in this field."

3. **Engage in Conversations**
Step-by-Step Guide:
   1. **Start with Your Prepared Questions:**

- **Task:** Use your prepared questions to start conversations with speakers and other attendees.

- **Tip:** Listen actively and show genuine interest in their responses.

   1. **Share Your Contact Information:**

- **Task:** Offer your business card or share your digital business card during the conversation.

- **Tip:** Follow up with the contacts you make after the conference.

Virtual Participation

Not everyone can travel to every conference. Luckily, virtual attendance is now common, especially since the pandemic. Attending a conference from your living room might not be as exciting as being there in person, but it's still very effective. Treat it like an in-person event: schedule time for sessions, avoid distractions and participate actively. Many platforms let virtual attendees ask questions or join discussions, so get involved. The more engaged you are, the more you'll learn.

Use the available tools. Use chat functions to ask speakers questions, join breakout rooms if available, and participate in polls or surveys. Some conferences also offer virtual networking, connecting you with other attendees based on shared interests. It's like speed dating but for knowledge and insights.

Post-Conference Learning

The end of the conference isn't the end of your learning. It's just the beginning. Gather the business cards and notes you've collected and start following up. Reach out to your new contacts with a personalized note, maybe mentioning a conversation you had or a session you both attended. This can turn brief encounters into lasting professional relationships.

Review your notes and identify key takeaways. Think about how they can be applied to your work or studies. Look for post-conference materials like recordings or slide shares if you missed any sessions. Many conferences provide these resources, which can be invaluable for catching up or deepening your understanding.

AI conferences are dynamic and exciting, full of learning and networking opportunities. Whether you're a first-timer or a seasoned attendee, each conference helps you understand AI better, meet like-minded professionals, and get inspired by new innovations. So, get ready for the next AI conference. The insights you gain could spark your next big project, career move, or breakthrough. And who knows? In a few years, it might be you on that stage, sharing your contributions with eager attendees from around the world.

7.5 Reading List: Essential Books on AI for Continuous Learning

Books are like trusty maps guiding you through the world of AI. A good reading list can help you go from a beginner to an expert. Let's build that bridge from curiosity to knowledge, one book at a time.

Start with the basics. These "AI 101" books are essential for every enthusiast. Think of them as your base camp for climbing the AI mountains. "Artificial Intelligence: A Guide for Thinking Humans" by Melanie Mitchell gives an excellent overview of AI, perfect for grounding your understanding. "AI Superpowers" by Kai-Fu Lee shows how AI shapes the world, especially in the U.S. and China. It's like having a guide showing you the ropes in the global AI arena.

As you get more comfortable, dive deeper into how AI works. "Deep Learning" by Ian Goodfellow, Yoshua Bengio, and Aaron Courville is like a detailed map through the complex world of neural networks and machine learning. It's not light reading, but it's very thorough. For those interested in the ethical side of AI, "Weapons of Math Destruction" by Cathy O'Neil explores how AI impacts real lives. It's a must-read for understanding the broader implications of AI.

Stay updated with periodicals and journals like "Journal of Artificial Intelligence Research" or "AI Magazine." These inform you about the latest research and discussions in the AI community, offering a mix of in-depth articles and case studies. It's like having a subscription to the latest in the AI world.

Balance your reading list. Dive deep into the technical aspects of AI, but also understand its applications and implications. Include books on AI's impact on society, ethics, and future job markets, like "The Big Nine" by Amy Webb, which looks at how AI could evolve in the coming decades. Also, read novels featuring AI to spark your imagination, like "Neuromancer" by William Gibson, a classic that has inspired many.

Building your AI reading list is like stocking a toolkit; each book offers unique tools and perspectives, helping you tackle AI from all angles. Whether you're looking to understand machine learning algorithms or the ethical dilemmas of AI, there's a book for you. Keep reading, keep learning, and let each page turn fuel your journey into AI.

7.6 The Role of Podcasts in AI Education

Podcasts are a great way to learn about AI while doing other things like jogging, washing dishes, or commuting. They are like friendly professors who make complex AI ideas easy to understand without needing a textbook. Popular AI podcasts like "AI in Business" and "The AI Alignment Podcast" offer deep dives into how AI is transforming industries and the ethical issues it raises. "The Lex Fridman Podcast" features interviews with AI experts, giving you new perspectives on the AI landscape. Think of these podcasts as your ongoing AI seminar, available anytime, right in your earbuds.

Listening to podcasts during your daily routine can be a game-changer. Multitasking is only sometimes effective, but it's a win when you listen to an AI podcast while doing something mundane. Whether on your morning jog or stuck in traffic, these moments can become productive learning opportunities. It's like having a floating classroom around you. Pick a consistent time for listening—maybe during your morning coffee or while winding down in the evening. The key is consistency. Over time, these learning snippets add up, giving you a wealth of knowledge without feeling like you're squeezing in extra study time.

Podcasts do more than inform; they humanize AI. Hearing experts talk about their work, challenges, and predictions makes AI feel less distant and more like a field shaped by real people. This helps bridge the gap between abstract concepts and real-world applications. Podcasts complement your formal AI education by connecting the dots between theory and practice. Hearing how theories play out in actual scenarios or understanding the thought process of someone deep in AI development can illuminate your textbook learning in surprising ways.

Engage with the communities around these podcasts. Many have listener groups on social media or forums where fans discuss episodes, share insights, and pose questions. Joining these communities is like attending the after-party of a conference where you chat with other attendees, share notes, and deepen your understanding of the talks. Engaging with these communities encourages active learning—discussing and questioning what you learn rather than passively consuming information.

Podcasts, with their blend of accessibility and informal learning, are a powerful tool in your AI education. They offer a unique way to stay updated, deepen your understanding, and connect with the AI community without feeling overwhelmed. They show that learning can be informal yet enriching, fitting seamlessly into your daily life. So, next time you plug in your headphones, remember that each episode expands your mind.

Keeping up with AI isn't just about chasing information. It's about strategically choosing and integrating your learning tools to make learning continuous, enjoyable, and enriching. Podcasts are just one part of this ongoing learning journey, blending into your daily routines and providing a window into the expansive world of AI. Next, we'll explore how to take this learning into the real world, applying AI knowledge practically and impactfully. Stay tuned; the adventure continues!

Chapter 7 Exercises:

Exploring Subreddits on Reddit

Objective: Understand how to use subreddits on Reddit to explore specific topics, interests, or themes.

Instructions:

1. **Sign Up for a Reddit Account**

Step-by-Step Guide:
  1. **Create an Account:**

- **Task**: Go to Reddit and sign up for a free account.

- **Steps:**

1. Click "Sign Up" in the top-right corner.

2. Enter your email address and choose a username and password.

3. Complete the verification process.

2. Identify Your Interests
Step-by-Step Guide:
  1. **List Your Interests:**

- **Task**: Write down a list of topics you are interested in.

- **Examples**:

- Artificial Intelligence

- Cooking

- Gardening

- Fitness

- Technology

3. Find Relevant Subreddits
Step-by-Step Guide:
  1. **Search for Subreddits:**

- **Task**: Use the search bar at the top of the Reddit homepage to find subreddits related to your interests.

- **Steps**:

1. Type a keyword from your list of interests into the search bar (e.g., "Artificial

Intelligence").

2. Review the suggested subreddits and select ones that match your interest.

3. **Join Subreddits**:

- **Task**: Click on the subreddit names to visit their pages and join the ones you like.

- **Steps**:

1. Click the "Join" button to subscribe on the subreddit page.

2. Repeat for other subreddits that interest you.

Examples of Popular Subreddits:

- Artificial Intelligence: r/artificial

- Machine Learning: r/MachineLearning

- Cooking: r/Cooking

- Gardening: r/Gardening

- Fitness: r/Fitness

4. Explore and Engage
Step-by-Step Guide:

1. **Browse Content**:

- **Task**: Spend some time browsing the posts in your joined subreddits.

- **Tip**: Look for posts that interest you and read through the comments to understand the community.

1. **Engage with Posts:**

- **Task**: Upvote interesting posts, leave comments, and participate in discussions.

- **Tip**: Be respectful and follow the subreddit's rules and guidelines.

5. Create a Post

Step-by-Step Guide:

1. **Make Your First Post:**

- **Task**: Create a post in one of your joined subreddits.

- **Steps**:

1. Go to the subreddit where you want to post.

2. Click the "Create Post" button.

3. Write a title and the content of your post.

4. Add any relevant tags or flair if required.

5. Click "Post" to share it with the community.

Example Post Ideas:

- **Question**: "What are the latest trends in Artificial Intelligence?"

- **Discussion**: "How do you incorporate AI in your daily work?"

- **Share**: "Check out this article on AI in healthcare!"

Summary

By following these steps, you can effectively explore and engage with subreddits on Reddit, expanding your knowledge and connecting with communities that share your interests. This beginner-friendly Exercise will help you become familiar with how subreddits work and how to use them effectively.

Chapter Eight

Leveraging AI for Future Opportunities

CHAPTER 8

Imagine walking into a world where your job isn't just about moving up step by step, but like getting on a super-fast elevator that takes you to places you never knew existed. Welcome to the exciting world of AI and machine learning careers! Think of this chapter as your special map, showing you all the cool places in AI, pointing out the best spots, and helping you find hidden treasures.

***

8.1 Career Paths in AI and Machine Learning

Cool AI Careers

Let's talk about some exciting careers. Not just any jobs, but the ones that seem like they're straight out of a sci-fi movie. From data scientists who analyze numbers to find patterns to AI researchers who are pushing the limits of what machines can learn, AI is packed with opportunities that were barely imaginable a decade ago. And don't forget about the AI application developers. These smart folks turn complex algorithms into user-friendly apps that even your grandma can use to check the weather or play her favorite songs.

What You Need to Start

What does it take to get into these cool jobs? First, you need some essential skills. In the AI world, this means knowing programming languages like Python or R and understanding data analysis. Then there's machine learning – it's not just a trendy word but a crucial skill that teaches computers to learn from data and make decisions. Think of it like training your dog to fetch; it takes patience, repetition, and a good understanding of behaviors.

But it's not all about technical skills. Problem-solving and critical thinking are just as important. You'll often face tricky data puzzles that you'll need to solve with sharp thinking and a bit of creativity. And explaining your awesome AI model to someone who doesn't know much about AI is crucial. It's about making the complicated stuff simple and understandable.

New AI Jobs

There are some fascinating new AI roles, too. Have you heard of an AI ethicist? As AI becomes more common, it is becoming very important to ensure that these technologies are used responsibly. Then there are jobs like AI health informatics specialists, who use AI in healthcare to predict patient outcomes, personalize treatments, and even help find cures for diseases.

Lifelong Learning in AI

A career in AI means being a lifelong learner because the field changes fast. Keep your skills fresh with online courses, webinars, and workshops. Networking with people who share your interests can open doors to new opportunities. Think of each connection as a node in your professional network, helping you learn and grow.

AI Career Quiz

Curious about which AI career might suit you best? Take this quick quiz! Answer questions about your interests and skills to discover your potential AI career path. It's like one of those career aptitude tests in school, but way cooler.

Starting Your Own AI Business

If you want to start an AI-focused business, you need a plan. First, do market research to understand what people need and where your AI can help. Find your niche, whether it's improving cybersecurity, healthcare, or customer service.

Starting a business costs money, especially an AI business. You might need help from investors or grants. Pitching your AI startup means showing potential financial returns and a deep understanding of AI's capabilities and limitations. It's about painting a picture of a future improved by your product.

Steering your way through the AI career landscape can be as thrilling as rewarding. Whether you're deciphering data, teaching machines to learn, or ensuring AI ethics are upheld, the opportunities are as vast as your imagination. So grab your gear, sharpen those skills, and prepare to explore the exciting world of AI and machine learning careers. Who knows? Your dream job is waiting at the intersection of curiosity and technology.

8.2 Starting Your Own AI Business

Imagine you're at a carnival, but instead of games, booths are showing off the latest AI inventions. Each inventor excitedly explains how their creation will change the world. That's what the AI startup scene is like—busy, lively, and full of promise.

AI startups often combine clever ideas with real-world solutions. For example, one startup made an AI tool to save energy in buildings, cutting costs and reducing pollution.

Another created a chatbot that answers medical questions, books appointments, and checks symptoms. These businesses solve real problems with AI.

Starting an AI business could be your next big adventure. First, you need a plan—like a treasure map. In business, this means doing market research to understand what people need and where your AI can help. Find your niche, whether it's improving cybersecurity, healthcare, or customer service.

Next, you need funding. Starting a business can be expensive, especially for an AI startup. You might need help from investors or grants. To get funding, you must show potential financial returns and a deep understanding of what your AI can do. It's about painting a picture of a future made better by your product.

Starting a business has challenges, like finding good data and following data privacy rules. However, these challenges can also be opportunities to show customers that their data is safe with you.

Exciting trends are shaping AI businesses. One trend is edge AI, which puts AI features directly into devices like smartphones, making them faster and more efficient. Another trend is using AI for sustainability, like managing energy use and waste. These trends offer lots of opportunities for new businesses.

As you prepare for the AI startup world, remember that creativity, resilience, and understanding AI's potential are your best tools. Whether you're streamlining business processes or tackling societal challenges, the journey from idea to market leader is both challenging and exciting. So, put on your inventor's hat and start planning your AI-driven future—it's a wild ride worth taking!

8.3 AI for Lifelong Learning and Personal Growth

Imagine you're back in school, but instead of heavy textbooks, you have AI helping you learn in the best way for you. Whether you learn best with videos or reading at your own pace, AI in education is like having a personal teacher ready to match your unique style. This is happening now and changing how we learn around the world.

AI-driven learning platforms use algorithms to see how you interact with the material. If you're struggling with calculus, the AI notices and offers extra help or simpler explanations until you get it. It's like having a tutor who helps you understand the material at your own pace.

Now, let's talk about the tools making this possible. AI tutors, virtual labs, and simulation software are revolutionizing learning. AI tutors give real-time feedback, guide you through problems, and adjust the difficulty level. Virtual labs let you do experiments without a physical lab. Imagine doing a chemistry reaction from your kitchen table! Simulation software lets you practice things like flying a plane or performing surgery safely.

To get the most out of these AI tools, start integrating them into your digital experiences. AI-powered browsers and search engines can make online learning more efficient and safe. Many educational websites now use AI to provide tailored learning experiences, so explore these resources.

AI isn't just changing education; it's also helping with career growth. Staying competitive means keeping up with the latest technologies. AI-driven platforms can help you learn new skills and update old ones. AI certifications and courses are gateways to staying relevant in a fast-changing job market. Many platforms use AI to match learning paths with career goals, providing a personalized roadmap to achieve your aspirations.

Balancing AI with human skills is crucial. While AI can analyze data quickly, it can't replace creative thinking or emotional intelligence. Skills like creativity, leadership, empathy, and communication make you stand out. These human-centric skills are more important than ever, fueling innovation and driving businesses forward.

As AI evolves, integrating it into your personal and professional development isn't just an option; it's necessary to stay ahead. But remember, it's about using AI to enhance your learning experience and career opportunities while nurturing the human skills that make you unique. Whether you're a student, a professional, or a lifelong learner, AI offers a path to thrive in the modern world. So, embrace AI and develop those human qualities that no algorithm can replicate.

8.4 How AI Is Shaping the Future of Industries

The Future with AI

Imagine walking down the busy streets of future industries. AI isn't just there; it's the mastermind reshaping everything. From healthcare to finance and retail to manufacturing, AI is like a supercharged builder, making operations smoother, improving customer interactions, and even changing what it means to work. So, put on your hard hat, and let's explore this changing world.

AI in Healthcare

In healthcare, AI is doing more than crunching numbers; it's saving lives. Picture a world where your smartwatch can predict a heart attack before it happens and alert your doctor in real time. This isn't sci-fi; it's real. AI analyzes tons of medical data to find patterns humans might miss. Hospitals use AI robots in surgeries, offering precision that even the best human hands can't match. These advancements are making healthcare proactive, focusing on prevention and treatment.

AI in Finance

In finance, AI is like a super-smart calculator and a crystal ball. AI algorithms can detect fraudulent transactions in milliseconds, much faster than humans. In trading, AI analyzes global financial news instantly and predicts stock movements quicker than any human trader. It's not just about automation; it's about making better decisions with insights from vast amounts of data. AI is like a meticulous analyst and an insightful adviser all in one.

AI in Retail

Imagine walking into a store where the shopping experience is made just for you, thanks to AI. Digital kiosks greet you by name, suggest products based on your shopping history, and even offer virtual try-ons. Behind the scenes, AI manages inventories in real time, predicting trends and optimizing stock levels to reduce waste. This personalized approach boosts sales and makes shopping more enjoyable. It's like having a personal shopper who knows what you want before you do.

AI in Manufacturing

In manufacturing, AI is like the conductor of an orchestra. It predicts machine malfunctions before they happen, minimizing downtime and maintenance costs. AI-driven robots work alongside humans, handling dangerous or tedious tasks and improving safety and efficiency. Integrating AI in manufacturing isn't about replacing humans but enhancing their abilities, allowing workers to focus on more complex and creative tasks. Here, AI is not just a tool but a teammate.

AI and Employment

AI's impact on jobs is significant. Yes, AI automates tasks, which can lead to some job losses. However, it also creates new roles and opportunities that require skills that are not yet mainstream. The workforce must adapt, learn new skills, and even re-skill to stay relevant. For example, as AI takes over routine data analysis, financial analysts can focus on strategy and advisory roles, requiring more analytical and interpersonal skills.

AI and Business Models

AI is leading the on-demand economy, where services and products are personalized and delivered when and where you want them. From streaming movies based on your preferences to healthcare apps that monitor your health and offer real-time advice, AI prioritizes convenience.

Preparing for AI Changes

Businesses and individuals need to be agile and continually learn to prepare for AI-driven changes. For businesses, this means investing in AI technologies and talent, fostering a culture of innovation, and adapting business models to leverage AI. For individuals, it means embracing lifelong learning, staying updated with technological advancements, and being open to new ways of working. Whether you're a CEO or a recent graduate, understanding AI's potential and implications for your industry is crucial.

The AI Future

The possibilities are endless and exciting as AI influences every job, process, and interaction. The future isn't just happening; it's being actively built with AI as both the blueprint and the builder. So, as you step into this brave new world, remember that adaptability and continuous learning are your best tools to thrive in an AI-enhanced future.

8.5: Preparing for a Future Dominated by AI

Embracing the AI Roller Coaster

Think of the future as a giant amusement park; AI is the intense roller coaster that flips you upside down and spins you around. Intimidating? Maybe. Exciting? Definitely. To enjoy the ride, you'll need the right mindset: an AI-ready mindset that embraces change and innovation, like a surfer riding the waves. It's about seeing change as an exciting challenge, not something to fear.

Being Flexible

Being flexible is key. Remember playing with Play-Doh as a kid? It could be anything—a snake, a cake, a race car. Be like Play-Doh: adaptable and ready to mold yourself into new roles and ideas as AI reshapes the world. Embrace lifelong learning because learning never stops in AI. It's like being in school forever, but in a good way, where every piece of knowledge adds another tool to your toolbox.

Learning Paths

Now, onto the practical stuff: learning paths. This isn't about a neat path; it's more like hacking through a jungle. You'll need technical skills—yes, coding might be necessary, but it's not as scary as it sounds. Think of it as learning a new language that lets you talk to computers. But it's not all about tech. Understanding the broader impact of AI on society and ethics is important too. It's like having a map that shows you where you're going and the pitfalls and scenic views along the way. Look for courses that teach you how to use AI tools and challenge you to think about how AI is used and its impact.

Staying Informed

Adapting to technological change is like building a plane while flying it. Sounds crazy, right? But with AI reshaping industries, that's what we're all doing. Staying informed is critical. Keep an eye on the latest AI developments, not just in your field but across the board. Follow tech news, read AI blogs, join forums, and tinker with AI software. It's like being a detective, always looking for clues about where AI is heading next. Be proactive in learning new tools and technologies. Don't wait for the future to come to you—go out and greet it with your handy new AI toolbox.

Building Resilience

Building resilience in a tech-driven world is crucial. It's easy to feel overwhelmed by keeping up with the latest technologies. Here's where resilience comes in. Think of it as your tech backbone; it helps you stand tall and confident, even when faced with rapid changes. Start by setting small, achievable goals. This could be learning one new AI concept weekly or building a small project every month. Celebrate these small victories; they're your stepping stones to mastering AI. And don't be afraid to fail. In the tech world, failures are as valuable as successes. They're opportunities to learn, grow, and become more resilient. Remember, every tech wizard has a trail of epic fails behind them.

Staying Human in a Tech World

As you prepare for a future dominated by AI, remember that it's not just about keeping up with the machines but also about staying human. It's about blending technical know-how with ethical considerations, creativity with code, and resilience with continuous learning. So, strap in, hold tight, and enjoy the ride—it's going to be wild!

***

8.6 Embracing AI: Next Steps in Your AI Journey

Dive Deeper into AI

So, you've started exploring AI and want to learn even more. Awesome! Think of AI as your new favorite hobby—fascinating, challenging, but totally exciting. Let's get practical with some steps to turn your AI curiosity into real skills.

Attend AI Workshops and Seminars

First, check out some AI workshops and seminars. These are like gym sessions for your brain. Just like you wouldn't run a marathon without training, you shouldn't dive into AI without some basic knowledge. Workshops are great because they offer hands-on experiences where making mistakes is part of the learning process. Look for local tech meetups, university lectures open to the public, or online webinars you can join from home. These sessions often introduce beginner-friendly AI concepts and tools, providing a safe space to ask questions.

Join Online AI Communities

Joining online AI communities can be super helpful, too. Think of these as virtual hangouts where everyone talks about AI. Platforms like Stack Overflow, GitHub, or specific Reddit forums can offer insights and answers from people who were once beginners like you. These communities are full of information where you can share your journey, get project feedback, or even find mentors. It's about building your AI network; these folks will cheer you on, offer advice, and share resources to help you grow.

Start a Small AI Project

Here's the fun part—start a small AI project. Nothing teaches better than doing it yourself. It could be as simple as using an AI-powered app to manage your daily tasks or as ambitious as building a simple chatbot. The key is to apply what you're learning in real-world scenarios. Remember, it's okay if these projects aren't perfect. Every mistake helps you understand AI better.

Use the Right Resources

Having the right tools can make learning AI easier. For your ongoing AI education, here are some resources you should check out:

1. Online Courses: Websites like Coursera and edX offer courses on everything from Python programming to neural networks. These platforms often feature courses developed by universities and tech companies, so you get top-notch information.

2. Books: Grab essential reads like "Artificial Intelligence: A Guide for Thinking Humans" by Melanie Mitchell or "Superintelligence" by Nick Bostrom. These books provide great insights into AI's capabilities and future.

3. Podcasts: Tune into shows like "AI in Business" or "The AI Alignment Podcast." These can be great companions during your commute, offering the latest discussions in the world of AI.

4. Forums and Communities: Join AI-focused forums on platforms like LinkedIn or specialized web communities. They can be invaluable for networking and staying updated on AI trends.

Experiment with AI

I encourage you to experiment. AI is a field driven by innovation and experimentation. The more you play with AI tools, the more you understand their potential and limitations. Whether tweaking a data model or automating part of your daily tasks, each experiment will add to your understanding of AI.

Embrace AI in Daily Life

As you weave these practices into your daily and professional life, you'll notice how AI isn't just a study subject but a tool that can enhance your productivity, creativity, and decision-making. The future of AI offers a landscape of opportunities, and by taking these steps, you're not just watching the future happen; you're actively participating in shaping it.

Wrapping Up

Remember, your AI adventure is just beginning. The steps and resources I've shared here are your map and compass, guiding you through the exciting terrain that AI presents. With each step, you're not just learning about AI; you're preparing yourself to be a part of a future where AI is as commonplace as smartphones. So keep exploring, experimenting, and, most importantly, enjoying the journey into the AI world.

Chapter 8 - Exercises

Exercise 1: Incorporating AI into Your Browser

1. **Installing an AI-Powered Browser Extension:**
   1. **Choose a Browser Extension:**

   - Pick an AI-powered extension to improve your browsing (e.g., Grammarly for grammar checking, Pocket for content recommendations).

   1. **Install the Extension**:

   - Install it in your favorite browser (e.g., Chrome, Firefox, Safari, and Arc).

   - **Explore Its Features**

   - Write a summary of how it improves your browsing experience.

2. **Practical Application:**
   1. **Use the AI-powered browser extension for a week**

   - Use the AI-powered extension for a week. Notice any changes in productivity or browsing experience.

   1. **Share Your Observations:**

   - Write a brief report on the benefits or challenges you encountered.

Exercise 2: Using AI in Email Writing (Outlook)

Setting Up AI Features in Outlook:
1. **Open Outlook:**

- Launch your Outlook app or log into the Outlook web version.

1. **Enable Copilot:**

- Click the Copilot icon in the upper-right corner. If you don't see it, update Outlook or check your subscription.

- Try prompts to get information, find files, or summarize emails in the Copilot pane.

1. **Using AI Features:**

- **Drafting Emails:** Start typing your email. Copilot will help draft it, adjust the tone, and length.

- **Real-Time Editing**: Copilot suggests grammar, punctuation, and style improvements.

- **Email Summaries**: Copilot summarizes long email threads for quick understanding and effective responses.

Practical Application:
1. **Enable and Use Copilot for a Week:**

- Use features like email drafting and summarizing for all your emails over a week.

1. **Reflection:**

- Reflect on your experience. Did the AI features save you time? Did they help improve your emails? Write a summary of your observations.

For a step-by-step video guide, you can watch this helpful YouTube video on setting up AI features in Outlook.

Exercise 3: Starting a Small AI Project

1. Choosing a Project:
   1. **Select a Project:**

   - Pick a small AI project, like creating a chatbot or analyzing a dataset using a basic AI model.

2. Planning and Execution:
   1. **Outline the Steps:**

   - Plan the steps to complete your project. What tools will you use? What data or resources do you need?

   1. **Execute Your Project:**

   - Follow your plan to complete the project.

Exercise 4: Exploring AI Resources

1. Online Courses:
   1. **Sign Up for an AI Course:**

   - Sign up for an introductory AI course on platforms like Coursera or edX.

   1. **Complete the First Module:**

   - Write a summary of what you learned.

2. Joining an Online Community:
   1. **Join an AI Community:**

   - Join an AI-focused online community, like a Reddit forum or a LinkedIn group.

Exercise 5: Understanding the Broader Impact of AI

1. **Research Task:**
    1. **Research AI in an Industry:**

        - Research how AI transforms a specific industry (e.g., healthcare, finance, retail, manufacturing).

    2. **Ethics and AI:**
    1. **Read or Watch About AI Ethics:**

        - Read an article or watch a video about AI ethics.

By completing these exercises, you will gain hands-on experience with AI in various aspects of life. You'll be better prepared for the exciting opportunities and challenges AI presents.

Keeping the Learning Alive

Now that you've explored the world of AI and have all the tools you need to start using it in your life, it's time to share what you've learned with others! Just like you found this book helpful, there are others out there who are searching for the same kind of guidance.

Your experience could be the very thing that helps someone else take their first step into the exciting world of AI.

So, here's a small request:

Please leave a review for this book.

By sharing your thoughts, you're not just helping the next reader—you're keeping the learning alive. Your review might inspire…

…one more student to explore new ideas. …one more parent to connect with their tech-savvy kid. …one more teacher to bring AI into the classroom. …one more curious mind to start an amazing journey.

It only takes a minute, but it can make a big difference. Plus, it's a great way to pass on the knowledge and excitement you've gained.

Simply scan the QR code below to leave your review:

[https://www.amazon.com/review/review-your-purchases/?asin=BOOKASIN]

Thank you for being a part of this learning adventure. I hope you continue to explore, discover, and share your newfound knowledge. Remember, the more we learn and share, the better we all become!

Your biggest fan, W.R. Lawrence

P.S. - Your review is like a high five to the next reader—letting them know they're in for something great!

Chapter Nine

AI Made Easy: Conclusion

Well, here we are at the end of our grand tour through the land of AI and ChatGPT. If you're feeling more intelligent, tech-savvy, or just amazed at how much you've learned, our journey together has succeeded. Remember when you first peeked into these pages? Perhaps you needed to be more sure of what AI and ChatGPT stood for. Look at you now—navigating neural networks, crafting clever prompts, and maybe even whispering sweet nothings to your new AI companions to see how they respond.

Throughout this book, we've taken baby steps and giant leaps—from understanding the very bones of AI to using ChatGPT to automate daily tasks and boost productivity. We've rolled up our sleeves and dived into hands-on projects that taught us the "how" and the "why" behind using AI in various facets of our lives, professionally and personally.

Let's remember that having a lot of power also means having a lot of responsibility. Our foray into ethical AI use in Chapter 6 was more than a high-minded discourse. It's about the real-world nitty-gritty of applying AI in ways that respect privacy, ensure fairness, and embody our values. Because technology reflects those who wield it—so let's be the good guys, shall we?

AI isn't just a tool; it's a partner in our relentless pursuit of innovation. It's there when we create, learn, and decide, enhancing our innate abilities and opening doors we didn't even know existed. Whether spinning up articles, managing our finances with uncanny insight, or supporting our educational endeavors, AI is the silent partner you didn't know you needed.

Continuous learning might seem daunting—AI technology moves faster than a caffeinated cheetah. But fear not! Staying current is part of the fun. Dive into online forums, attend workshops, and maybe even hit up a conference. Keep playing with new tools, testing out projects from Chapter 5, or come up with your own. Every step, every stumble, is part of your growth.

So, what's next? Start your own AI projects! Grab an idea, gather some data, and let those algorithms fly. It doesn't have to be perfect; it must be yours. Every line of code and every query you run is a building block in your AI journey.

As we look to the future, imagine the possibilities. AI is reshaping the world; you can be a part of that transformation. Whether you're streamlining work operations, crafting stories, or making everyday life a little easier, your newfound skills will put you at the forefront of change.

Reflecting on the time spent writing this book, I have hoped to demystify AI to make it accessible, understandable, and fun. I'm excited about the future of AI—about your future with AI. This isn't just about technology; it's about potential—yours, mine, and ours together in this ever-evolving digital universe.

So, as we wrap up, remember this isn't the end. It's just the beginning—the start of your adventure with AI. Keep learning, keep exploring, and above all, keep asking questions. Who knows what you'll discover next?

Chapter Ten

AI Workbook: Using AI in Everyday Tech Devices

Welcome to your journey with AI! This chapter will show you how to use AI in your daily life. From managing emails and browsing the web to using your smartphone and picking music, we'll help simplify your tasks and boost your productivity. Over the next six days, you'll learn tools and tasks you can use immediately. Get ready to see how AI can transform your daily activities!

Day 1: Email Automation with AI

Activity 1: Enhance Email Writing

- **How to Use**: Add AI tools like Grammarly to your email. These tools help improve grammar, style, and tone.

- **Why Use**: AI saves time and helps you write better emails. It can also set up automatic replies, prioritize emails, and remind you to follow up.

- *When to Use:*

- Daily Email Management: Use Grammarly to check emails before sending them.

- Scheduling: Use Boomerang to send emails at the best times.

- Inbox Management: Set up automatic replies for common questions.

Task: Set up automatic email responses using AI.

Tip: Check out these YouTube tutorials to learn how:

1. How to Use Grammarly AI to Improve Your Writing

2. See How Generative AI Can Help You Write Better Emails

Activity 2: Schedule Emails with Boomerang

- **How to Use**: Use Boomerang for Gmail to schedule emails to be sent at optimal times.

- **Why Use**: Scheduling emails ensures they are sent when they are most likely to be read, improving the chances of timely responses.

- **When to Use**:

  - **Follow-Up Reminders:** Schedule reminders for emails that require responses.

  - **Timed Delivery:** Send emails when recipients are most likely to check their inbox.

Task:

1. Compose an email that you need to follow up on.

2. Use Boomerang to schedule the email to be sent later.

3. Set a reminder to follow up if you don't receive a response.

Activity 3: Enhance Productivity with Microsoft Co-Pilot

- **How to Use**: Add Microsoft Co-Pilot to Outlook to help with email management. It can draft emails, suggest improvements, and summarize long threads.

- **Why Use**: Co-Pilot saves time and helps ensure your emails are clear and professional.

- **When to Use**:

    - **Drafting Emails**: Use Co-Pilot to draft professional emails quickly.

    - **Improving Clarity**: Use Co-Pilot's suggestions to refine your messages.

    - **Summarizing Threads**: Get summaries of long email chains for quick responses.

Day 2: Browsing Made Smarter

Activity 1: Curate Personalized Content

- **How to Use**: Install AI tools like Pocket or Feedly to curate content based on your interests.

- **Why Use**: AI helps you stay organized and find relevant content quickly.

- **When to Use**:

    - **Daily Reading**: Use Pocket to save and organize articles for later.

    - **Content Recommendations:** Use Feedly to get updates on topics you like.

Task:
- Pocket: Create an account, save articles, and organize them with tags.

- Feedly: Create an account, subscribe to feeds, and customize your feed.

Activity 2: Organize Bookmarks

AI WORKBOOK:USING AI IN EVERYDAY TECH DEVICES   141

- **How to Use**: To organize your bookmarks automatically, use an AI-powered browser extension like Raindrop.io. The extension can be installed from the respective browser's extension store. For Safari, a small Mac app is required to activate the extension.

- **Why Use**: AI tools help keep your bookmarks organized and easily accessible.

- **When to Use:**

    - Bookmark Management: Categorize and manage your bookmarks efficiently with AI suggestions.

Activity 3: Enhanced Browsing with AI

- **How to Use**: Integrate ChatGPT *Max AI* and, *Perplexity* into your browser for smarter browsing and content recommendations. Max AI is an extension in the Chrome store.

- **Why Use**: These tools provide real-time assistance, generate insights, and help understand complex topics, enhancing your browsing experience.

- **When to Use:**

    - **Real-time Assistance**: Use ChatGPT for article summaries and recommendations.

    - **In-depth Insights**: Utilize Max-AI to generate insights on at least one daily article.

    - **Complex Topics**: Leverage Perplexity to explore and understand complex topics or articles.

Day 3: AI on Your Phone

Activity 1: Use Personal Assistants

- **How to Use**: Use Siri or Google Assistant to set reminders, send messages, and get answers.

- **Why Use**: AI assistants simplify tasks and boost productivity.

- **When to Use**:

    - **Daily Scheduling**: Set reminders and manage your calendar.

    - **Information Retrieval**: Quickly find information on various topics.

Activity 2: Schedule Your Day

- **How to Use**: Use AI assistants to plan and optimize your daily schedule.

- **Why Use**: AI organizes your day efficiently so you don't miss important tasks.

- **When to Use**:

    - Day Planning: Set up your calendar with tasks and reminders.

Activity 3: Voice Commands for Navigation and Travel

- **How to Use**: Employ voice commands with your AI assistant to get directions, check traffic, and find nearby places.

- **Why Use**: AI assistants provide real-time updates and suggestions, making travel and navigation hassle-free.

- **When to Use**:

    - **Driving**: Get directions and traffic updates hands-free while driving.

    - **Exploring**: Find nearby restaurants, gas stations, and other points of interest with simple voice commands.

Activity 4: Smart Home Integration

AI WORKBOOK: USING AI IN EVERYDAY TECH DEVICES

- **How to Use**: Connect your AI assistant to smart home devices using voice commands to control lights, thermostats, and security systems.

- **Why Use**: Enhance convenience and security in your home with integrated AI controls.

- **When to Use**:

    - **Home Automation**: Adjust lighting, temperature, and security settings with your voice.

    - **Routine Management:** Set up automated routines like turning off lights and locking doors when you say "goodnight.

Day 4: Smart Music with Sonos

Activity 1: Voice Control Music

- **How to Use**: Use Alexa or Sonos ("Hey Sonos") to control your Sonos speakers by voice.

- **Why Use**: Voice control is hands-free for managing your music experience.

- **When to Use:**

    - **Hands-Free Music**: Ask Alexa to play music, adjust the volume, or skip tracks without using your hands.

Activity 2: Multi-Room Audio

- **How to Use**: The Sonos app creates a multi-room audio setup.

- **Why Use**: Enjoy synchronized music throughout your home for a seamless audio experience.

- **When to Use**:

    - Home Entertainment: Play your favorite playlist in every room for an immersive music experience.

Day 4: Personalized Greeting Cards

Activity 1: Create AI-Generated Cards

- **How to Use**: Use Blue Mountain to create personalized greeting cards for special occasions.

- **Why Use:** AI helps you write, design, and personalize cards quickly and easily.

- **When to Use**:

  ○ Special Occasions: Customize and send greeting cards for birthdays, holidays, and other events.

Activity 2: Schedule Card Deliveries

- **How to Use**: Use Blue Mountain Scheduler to schedule greeting cards to be sent on future dates.

- *Why Use:* Ensure timely delivery of greeting cards without manual intervention.

- **When to Use**:

- Event Planning: Schedule cards for future dates to remember important occasions.

Day 5: Creative Writing with AI: Composing Poetry and Stories

Activity 1: AI-Powered Story and Poetry Generation

- How to Use: Utilize tools like ChatGPT or Jasper AI to generate story ideas, write poetry, or create short stories. Input a prompt or theme, and let the AI assist in crafting your narrative.

- **Why Use:** AI can help overcome writer's block, offer unique ideas, and generate text that can serve as inspiration or a starting point for your writing.

- **When to Use:**

  - **Writing Exercises:** Use AI to kickstart creative exercises, such as generating the first few lines of a poem or a story's opening scene.

  - **Creative Projects:** Leverage AI when you need inspiration for larger writing projects or when you're exploring new genres or styles.

Activity 2: Style Mimicry and Experimentation

- **How to Use:** Use AI tools to experiment with different writing styles. You can input text in the style of famous authors or poets and let AI generate content that mimics those styles.

- **Why Use:** Experimenting with different writing styles can help you find your unique voice or understand the nuances of various literary techniques.

- **When to Use:**

  - **Literary Studies:** Enhance your understanding of different authors' styles by comparing AI-generated content with original works.

  - **Creative Exploration:** Experiment with writing in the style of different genres or authors to expand your creative range.

Activity 3: Real-Time Editing and Feedback

- **How to Use:** Use AI tools like Grammarly or ProWritingAid for real-time editing and feedback on your creative drafts. These tools can suggest improvements in grammar, style, and clarity.

- **Why Use:** Immediate feedback helps you refine your writing more efficiently, making editing smoother and less time-consuming.

- When to Use:

    - **Drafting:** Use AI to get real-time feedback as you write, ensuring your drafts are polished from the start.

    - **Final Revisions:** Before submitting or publishing your work, run it through AI tools for a final round of edits to catch any remaining issues.

Day 6: Creating Images with AI: A Beginner's Guide

Activity 1: Exploring AI Image Generation Tools

- How to Use: Start with DALL-E, Midjourney, or Stable Diffusion to create images based on text descriptions. Practice by describing simple scenes and gradually move to more complex visuals.

- Why Use: AI tools make it easy to visualize and create art, even if you have no traditional artistic skills.

- When to Use:

    - **Creative Projects:** Generate visuals for stories, presentations, or personal art projects.

    - **Learning:** Experiment with different tools to understand their capabilities and limitations.

Activity 2: Enhancing Creativity with AI

- How to Use: AI generates variations of a single concept or theme, helping you explore different creative directions.

- Why Use: AI can provide fresh perspectives and new ideas, sparking creativity and helping you think outside the box.

- When to Use:

    ◦ **Brainstorming Sessions:** Generate multiple image options to inspire new ideas or directions for your creative work.

    ◦ **Concept Development:** Use AI to visualize concepts during the early stages of a project, making it easier to refine and develop your ideas.

Activity 3: Practical Application and Sharing

- How to Use: After creating your images, use them in presentations, social media posts, or as part of a larger creative project. Share your work with others to receive feedback and inspire further creativity.

- Why Use: Applying your AI-generated images in real-world contexts helps you understand their impact and value, and sharing your work can lead to constructive feedback and new ideas.

- When to Use:

    ◦ **Portfolio Development:** Add AI-generated art to your creative portfolio to showcase your skills.

    ◦ **Collaborative Projects:** Use AI-generated images in group projects or collaborative creative efforts, blending human and AI creativity.

Summary

Using AI in your daily routine can make you more productive and make tasks easier. From automating email management and curating personalized content to using AI assistants on your phone and managing your music and greeting cards, these practical steps will help you make the most of AI technology starting today. Try these tools to see their benefits for yourself!

Chapter Eleven

References

Bullas, J. (n.d.). 7 Highly-Informative Websites to Stay Up-to-Date with the Latest AI Developments. Retrieved from https://www.jeffbullas.com/ai-news/

Codecademy. (n.d.). How to Setup a ChatGPT Account. Retrieved from https://www.codecademy.com/article/how-to-setup-a-chat-gpt-account

Digital Daze. (n.d.). Top 10 AI Budgeting Tools of 2024. Retrieved from https://digitaldaze.io/the-best-ai-budgeting-tools/

Dur, E. (2024, January 24). 6 Critical – And Urgent – Ethics Issues With AI. Forbes. Retrieved from https://www.forbes.com/sites/eliamdur/2024/01/24/6-critical–and-urgent–ethics-issues-with-ai/#:~:text=One%20of%20the%20foremost%20ethical,rigorous%20testing%20and%20continuous%20monitoring.

Exabeam. (n.d.). The Intersection of GDPR and AI and 6 Compliance Best Practices. Retrieved from https://www.exabeam.com/explainers/gdpr-compliance/the-intersection-of-gdpr-and-ai-and-6-compliance-best-practices/

Feedspot. (n.d.). Top 100 AI Influencers in 2024 (Artificial Intelligence). Retrieved from https://influencers.feedspot.com/artificial_intelligence_twitter_influencers/

Forbes Tech Council. (2023, November 28). Ensuring Data Privacy: 20 Best Practices For Businesses In The AI Age. Forbes. Retrieved from https://www.forbes.com/sites/forbestechcouncil/2023/11/28/ensuring-data-privacy-20-best-practices-for-businesses-in-the-ai-age/

Fortune. (n.d.). Here are 7 free AI classes you can take online from top tech firms and universities. Retrieved from https://fortune.com/education/articles/free-ai-classes-you-can-take-online/

REFERENCES

Google Cloud. (n.d.). Supervised vs. unsupervised learning: What's the difference? Retrieved from https://cloud.google.com/discover/supervised-vs-unsupervised-learning

Harvard Gazette. (2020, October). Ethical concerns mount as AI takes a bigger role in decision-making. Retrieved from

IBM. (n.d.). Shedding light on AI bias with real world examples. Retrieved from https://www.ibm.com/blog/shedding-light-on-ai-bias-with-real-world-examples/

IEEE Spectrum. (n.d.). How Artificial Intelligence Can Personalize Education. Retrieved from https://spectrum.ieee.org/how-ai-can-personalize-education

LinkedIn. (n.d.). Case Studies: Success Stories of AI in Project Management. Retrieved from https://www.linkedin.com/pulse/case-studies-success-stories-ai-project-management-underhill-ppm–axtmf

Marr, B. (2023, May 30). 10 Amazing Real-World Examples Of How Companies Are Using ChatGPT in 2023. Forbes. Retrieved from https://www.forbes.com/sites/bernardmarr/2023/05/30/10-amazing-real-world-examples-of-how-companies-are-using-chatgpt-in-2023/

McKinsey & Company. (n.d.). The future is now: Unlocking the promise of AI in industries. Retrieved from https://www.mckinsey.com/industries/automotive-and-assembly/our-insights/the-future-is-now-unlocking-the-promise-of-ai-in-industrials

Microsoft. (n.d.). AI for Beginners. Retrieved from https://microsoft.github.io/AI-For-Beginners/

Punktum. (n.d.). The Ultimate Checklist for an AI/ML Startup. Retrieved from https://punktum.net/insights/the-ultimate-checklist-for-a-startup-venturing-into-ai-machine-learning-projects/

Quartz. (n.d.). Ten ways to use ChatGPT in your daily life. Retrieved from https://qz.com/10-practical-uses-chatgpt-improve-yo-ai-bias-with-real-world-examples/

Shepherd, I. (2024, March 27). The Top AI Tools For Content Creators In 2024. Forbes. Retrieved from

Shelf.io. (n.d.). How to Create AI Transparency and Explainability to Build Trust. Retrieved from https://shelf.io/blog/ai-transparency-and-explainability

Simonite, T. (2023, March 3). The inside story of how ChatGPT was built from the people.... MIT Technology Review. Retrieved from https://www.technologyreview.com/2023/03/03/1069311/inside-story-oral-history-how-chatgpt-built-openai/

Tech.co. (n.d.). ChatGPT Errors: Why They Happen and How to Fix Them. Retrieved from https://tech.co/news/chatgpt-errors-how-to-fix-them

Whova. (n.d.). Top 40 AI Conferences to Attend in 2024. Retrieved from https://whova.com/blog/best-ai-conferences/

Writesonic. (n.d.). 215+ ChatGPT Prompts You Can't Miss To Try Out In 2024. Retrieved from https://writesonic.com/blog/chatgpt-prompts

Zapier. (n.d.). The best AI productivity tools in 2024. Retrieved from https://zapier.com/blog/

Printed in Great Britain
by Amazon